A Tapestry of Love:

The Spirituality of Caregiving

Daphne Reiley and Joseph LaGuardia

Reiley, Daphne and Joseph LaGuardia

A Tapestry of Love: The Spirituality of Caregiving
2nd Edition

Bibliography: p. 115

Categories: Religion/Spirituality

ISBN 978-1492938040

In memory of my father, who was caregiver to his family with intensity and grace.

JVL

To Ralph, Thomas, and Amelia for their steadfast love and affection – without it, I wouldn't be here!

DCR

Now as they went on their way, he entered a certain village, where a woman named Martha welcomed him into her home. She had a sister named Mary, who sat at the Lord's feet and listened to what he was saying. But Martha was distracted by her many tasks; so she came to him and asked, "Lord, do you not care that my sister has left me to do all the work by myself? Tell her then to help me." But the Lord answered her, "Martha, Martha, you are worried and distracted by many things; there is need of only one thing. Mary has chosen the good part, which will not be taken away from her."

Luke 10:38-42

Table of Contents

Acknowledgements

It takes a village to write a book. For that, we are deeply and profoundly indebted to our various families in the faith and support systems that aided and inspired us in the writing of *A Tapestry of Love*.

This includes the various communities of faith who have encouraged us along the way and the caregivers in those communities—our teachers and mentors who have persevered with faith, hope and love.

Joe is deeply grateful for Trinity Baptist Church, Conyers, Georgia; Clairmont Oaks and Briarcliff Oaks; and the McAfee School of Theology for creating the sacred spaces that nurtured the Spirit's presence, invoked God's voice, and inspired Words and proclamation that make such writing possible. The Bible is correct when it says that we are surrounded by so great a cloud of witnesses.

Daphne would like to share her gratitude for the graciousness, encouragement, healing, and comfort found within the communities of First Christian Church of Decatur (Disciples of Christ), Decatur, Georgia; Columbia Theological Seminary; Sandy Springs Christian Church, Sandy Springs, Georgia; Northlake Gardens Assisted Living and Arbor Terrace – Decatur.

We are also grateful for those who shared in our journey of writing and editing, including the Rev. Dr. James Brewer-Calvert for encouraging Daphne to write and for introducing us; Yolanda

Lewellyn for reading our introduction and first chapter so long ago; the Rev. Melissa Fain for reading and encouraging us to keep going with getting this book to market so she could buy one; Kristine Medea, LPC, BCETS for her constant, even urgent, encouragement, and our editor, Melissa Elliot. They have saved us many an error; any that remain are our own.

Lastly, we would like to thank our families for their support, encouragement, patience and prayers through the four-year journey it took to write this book. We are especially thankful for our spouses, Ralph Reiley and Kristina LaGuardia, who have put up with our endless meetings, correspondences, and off-beat humor. Our children have also endured our pilgrimage, and have remained sources of inspiration on more than one occasion.

Introduction

From where Joe stands on his front porch, he can look down his quiet, suburban street and spot four homes in which the act of caregiving is taking place. Residents remodeled two homes to allow aging parents to move in with them. In a third home, a wife is taking care of her terminally-ill husband. The other is occupied by an octogenarian whose neighbor happens to be her daughter, her primary caregiver.

This is not a unique neighborhood. The population of caregivers is growing every day and has become a mainstay in American culture. One statistic claims that 29% of the U.S. population consists of caregivers.[1] Additionally, as the economy lumbers along and the costs of healthcare increase, more people are relying on one another for receiving and giving care. This adds stress to fragile family situations; caregiver burdens (as clinicians call them) begin to mount. It is reasonable to assume that we are indeed living in an age of caregiving.

As a result of this caregiver boom, resources, from books to websites, provide caregivers with strategies on how to cope with these burdens. Very few resources, however, connect caregivers with the ebb and flow of the Holy Spirit's movement in their

---

[1] "Fact Sheet: Selected Caregiver Statistics," *Family Caregiver Alliance*, online: http://www.caregiver.org/caregiver/jsp/contentnode.jsp?nodeid=439&expandnodeid=480 (accessed 13 October 2013).

lives. Not many people realize just how much the act of caregiving can shape a caregiver's spirituality, and vice versa. In *A Tapestry of Love*, we hope to connect caregivers with spiritual practices that have bolstered an ancient, still vibrant Christian faith.

Ω

The truth is that we are all caregivers and care receivers. We are all readers and writers, priests and ministers. We are sons and daughters, parents and siblings. We are spouses and friends. We all weave together a community that is on a journey, a journey in which our very lives intersect and create a tapestry of love that includes caregiving and faith.

When we look on the surface of our lives, all we see are the broken threads and loose strands of a fractured spiritual life. There is a great disconnect among the fibers of our being. This is because caregiving pulls us in so many directions and places us in so many roles. It consumes us and divides our attention.

When we care for others, it becomes hard to care for ourselves. Soon, we discover that we only exist as broken bread—broken bread given to and consumed by others. Expectations, schedules, routines, and pressures increase; we fail to pause and find nourishment from a connection with the One who was broken for us so long ago on Calvary.

Ultimately, connecting a caregiver with the deeper tapestry of love requires us to weave the various fragments and loose strands into a strong, united fabric that affirms one's relationship with God and with others. We hope to inspire you, as well as those who receive care, to participate in a journey to greater communion with Jesus Christ.

We invite professional caregivers, those who work in hospitals, hospices, and as in-home aids, along as well. We invite informal caregivers, those people called to care for aging parents, spouses, special-needs loved ones, and friends. Mind you, we do not limit our invitation to these groups. Anyone interested in spiritual growth is welcome to join in the pilgrimage and find a home between the covers of this book.

Ω

Several assumptions support this work. We assume that the act of caregiving and a caregiver's spiritual life relate to and inform one another. Caregiving is about nurturing. Spirituality is about nurturing. Caregiving concerns itself with relationships. Spirituality is about relationships. Caregiving is about life. Spirituality is about life. Caregiving and spirituality relate so closely that we can safely assert that our ability to manage the demands of our own spiritual needs determines how well we manage the demands of caregiving.

We also assume that God designs every human to be a spiritual and spirit-filled creature (Gen. 1:24-27). We are earthen vessels that require God's everlasting water, God's very Spirit, to quench our spiritual longing. Only when our cup overflows

4

with grace and forgiveness can we obtain the energy necessary to care for others.

As caregivers, we realize that no single day is the same as any other. Certainly, there are ways in which we successfully handle the daily stress that results from caregiving. Yet it becomes important to question whether the means by which we attend to our spiritual life are nurturing us and our care receivers.

Do we have the type of commitment to spiritual formation that inspires growth in our relationships with our care receiver and the Lord? Is that formation giving us what we need to live a whole and healthy life? Is it giving us what we need to anticipate and eventually greet the death of our care receiver, or even our own death? These are difficult questions, but important nonetheless.

We assume that we do not go it alone, but with the help of God's guiding Spirit and with others. In the very first pages of the Bible, we read about the transformative relationship between God and all humanity. There, at the beginning of time itself, God's creative Spirit—God's *ru'ah* or breath—moved upon the earth, gathered earth, and breathed life into it. This life was a mirror image of God. That Spirit is the same one that fills us to this day and beckons us homeward to the nurturing embrace of our Creator. Caregivers—thirsty and hungry from a long day of caring for others—are in need of this creative, life-giving Spirit. We all long for God's *ru'ah* to fill us once again with life and light for a new day.

Ω

We have a heart for caregivers because we have been caregivers and work with caregivers on a regular basis. We commit to walking with you in your own journey of faith. In her book, *Soul Feast*, Marjorie Thompson writes,

> *God's economy is not based on scarcity. The richest sources of spiritual nurture are permanently set upon the table of our lives. While it would be folly to ignore or refuse them, there is no need to rush or grab. Take and receive as you have need. Enjoy each to the full.*[2]

She states further,

> *God-in-Christ has received us into his own dwelling place, where we find in plenty all we have need of forgiveness, healing, reconciliation, comfort, peace, joy, communion – abundant life for body and soul. Could there be any hospitality to match that of the Host of Heaven?*[3]

It is this Host of Heaven that invites all of us — you, as reader, and us, as authors — to the table now.

This invitation to the table and this image of communion are important to Daphne. It was communion that renewed her Christian faith. Daphne's mother passed away in December of 2006

---

[2] Marjorie Thompson, *Soul Feast* (Louisville: Westminster John Knox Press, 1995), 154.

[3] Ibid., 131.

from complications with Alzheimer's disease. Her mother's journey with Alzheimer's began in earnest in 2000; and since that time, Daphne was her caregiver and her conservator. Most of all, Daphne was simply her daughter, even after her mother had forgotten that fact.

Toward the end of her mother's life, the Holy Spirit led Daphne to bring her mother spiritual sustenance in the form of that beautiful meal we Christians share — the bread and wine of communion. In doing so, Daphne was introduced to and joined the Disciples of Christ denomination.

As a community of faith, the Disciples of Christ denomination celebrates the Lord's Supper weekly. At first, Daphne found that rather disconcerting since she came from Presbyterian and Lutheran church traditions. However, she came to believe that the presence of Christ in that meal, shared with a communion of saints, was the source of the healing for her grief and separation from God.

In August of 2009, First Christian Church of Decatur (Disciples of Christ) commissioned the Caregiver Spiritual Support Ministry and installed Daphne as its director. Since its inception, she has recruited and trained prayer partners for the caregivers in the congregation. Those prayer partners supported caregivers by the act of spiritually listening to them and lifting their concerns, joys, and successes to God in unceasing prayer. Daphne has led prayer retreats as well as workshops.

Daphne's experience leads her to believe that caregiving was a holistic endeavor, necessarily making the art of caring for caregivers a holistic endeavor as well. Practicing the spiritual disciplines is just one way for the different threads of caregiving to be supported, and for caregivers to grow in faithfulness. Without the structure—without a working "loom"—of spiritual disciplines supporting us, guiding us, and weaving our spirituality into a strong tapestry, we could not keep up with the depth of the commitment needed to continue our work.

Ω

Joe started a ministry with caregivers shortly after becoming associate pastor of Trinity Baptist Church in Conyers, Georgia, in 2004. Trinity had always been a church of caregivers, a congregation that cared for loved ones, special needs children, spouses, aging parents and friends in the community. It was in that same year that the staff identified over a dozen caregivers in the small congregation, and Joe re-established fellowship groups for this segment of the church.

By 2006, Joe entered a doctoral degree program and focused on caregivers for his thesis project. That project eventually birthed the Center for Caregiver Spirituality, a ministry that offered support groups and an online web presence to caregivers in the community.

Ω

Perhaps some of these terms, such as *spiritual formation* or *spiritual disciplines* or *spiritual practices* are new to you, but they are historic aspects of the Christian life. Author and theologian, Robert Mulholland, defines spiritual formation as "the process of being conformed to the image of Christ for the sake of others."[4] This process helps us grow closer to God and mature in faith.

We grow closer to God *for the sake of others*. That means that our ministry to others—the actual work of caregiving—informs who we become in our relationship to Christ. Spiritual formation, in effect, works like a beating heart. While spiritual disciplines or practices help us take in "old blood" to renew its oxygen and strengthen nutrient levels, the "new blood" that goes forth from a healthy heart (ministry) strengthens our care of others.

The First (Old) Testament explains numerous situations in which spiritual formation occurred. The book of Psalms, for instance, reveals just how deeply the Israelites engaged in public and private spiritual practices. One of the most beloved Psalms, the twenty-third Psalm, expresses one's spiritual journey through God's greenest pasture, the darkest valley, and the heartiest banquet. The twenty-second Psalm, on the other hand, records a spiritual journey through God's absence and dark night of the soul.

---

[4] Robert Mulholland, *Invitation to a Journey: A Road Map for Spiritual Formation* (Downers Grove: InterVarsity Press, 1993), 12.

Israel's commitment to spiritual formation continued into the Second (New) Testament. Throughout the gospels, Jesus engaged various spiritual practices in order to balance his public ministry with self-care. Jesus knew that the only way to meet the needs of others was to allow his *Abba* (meaning, "father" or "daddy") to meet his spiritual needs.

Jesus also commanded his disciples to engage in a variety of spiritual practices, such as stewardship (Matthew 6:1-2), prayer (Matthew 6:5-6), and fasting (Matthew 6:16-18). The early church did just that: prayer, communion, and other spiritual disciplines were priorities for corporate (community) and individual growth (Acts 2:42).

In our own time, it is quite easy to find a church in which parishioners practice these and other historic spiritual disciplines. This book intends to add to the conversation about how spiritual disciplines play an important role in spiritual formation as it relates specifically to caregivers.

For the purpose of this book, the phrases "spiritual discipline" and "spiritual practice" are used interchangeably. In the more literal sense of the meaning, however, a discipline refers to a practice that someone or some community accomplishes or does over time. Although there is an adage that "practice makes perfect," we know that spiritual practices are those that can rarely be perfected. We discipline ourselves to engage in various practices even when we fail to benefit from them immediately or in the short-term. (A listing and explanation of historic spiritual practices can be found in Appendix A.)

Spiritual practices can form a loom for weaving a strong tapestry of love. What does a loom do? A loom guides the interweaving of the different strands of thread into a strong fabric. Depending on the characteristics of each unique strand of thread, the result will have its own unique strengths. The loom provides the basic structure, but the threads provide the intimate beauty to the fabric.

Since the time of the earliest desert mothers and fathers of the church, Christians have put into place a sort of spiritual loom that allows individuals to weave together a life of spiritual practice. This loom, often called a "rule of life," established a rhythm and structure for one's spiritual walk. The earliest formal rule came into existence in a monastic community led by St. Benedict. His rule, not only for his own life, but for the monks and nuns under his leadership, became and remains a benchmark for the Catholic Church. Even today, many religious communities—Catholic and otherwise—live under the Benedictine Rule, or one of its derivatives.

Looking at the analogy of the loom, we could say that the loom—a rule for our life—is similar. When we take the time to develop a rule for our life, we begin the construction of the loom.

At the outset, the loom has to be fed threads with which to do its weaving. As the fabric begins to be formed, the progress makes sense. The same is true with the spiritual disciplines and our practice of them. Each day we live with our rule is a thread fed into the loom.

So, let us look at the spiritual practices we have described above as threads for our loom. Just like working with a loom, the practices will appear bulky and will seemingly overpower our initial attempts at spiritual formation. At first, setting the threads and working the shuttle is a lot of work and takes practice in order to gain ease in the process. As our journey continues and growth happens, spiritual formation slowly can stand on its own, gathering its own nourishment and providing strength and shelter for us.

As that happens, the loom will recede but will always remain available as a tool. We never outgrow spiritual practices. Admittedly, there will be times when certain spiritual practices provide more of what we need than others, and that is perfectly acceptable. Changing patterns in the fabric of our spiritual lives gives variety and adds strength. Over time, they create a healthy and liberating tapestry that increases our love for the Lord and for others.

Chapter 1: Journey to Wholeness

*Now as they went on their way, he entered
a certain village, where a woman named
Martha welcomed him into her home. She
had a sister named Mary, who sat at the
Lord's feet and listened to what he was
saying. But Martha was distracted by her
many tasks; so she came to him and asked,
"Lord, do you not care that my sister has
left me to do all the work by myself? Tell
her then to help me." But the Lord
answered her, "Martha, Martha, you are
worried and distracted by many things;
there is need of only one thing. Mary has
chosen the good part, which will not be
taken away from her" (Luke 10:38-42).*

An Ancient Story

There she is! Mary is standing at the
doorway yet again. Does she think that Jesus will
come sooner if she continues to stare down the road?

Part of me wishes Jesus would not get here
until much later. There is so much to do.

"Mary!" She doesn't even hear me. She
never hears me.

"Mary!" Finally, she's pulling herself away
from that door. I believe I've caught her eye. "Mary,
we have much to do before Jesus and his friends get

here. Please help me! Shake the mats and fill the water jars. Perhaps Lazarus can help you with that.

"And herbs! I need herbs. Let's see; I need thyme, rosemary, dill, maybe some mint, too. Do we still have cumin in the spice cabinet?"

I see her moving towards the garden, and I am relieved to finally get some help. I wonder where Lazarus is. . . .

How long have I been standing in this heat? I'm hot from the soles of my feet to the top of my head. These ovens are full and working well, but it is so hot. Thanks be to God that the ovens are doing their job!

And the meal! The meal is going to be so delicious. I know Jesus and his friends will arrive tired and hungry, and I so love being able to prepare food that I know Jesus will enjoy.

I wonder what Mary and Lazarus have gotten into. Is that laughter I hear?

Wait. That smell. The rosemary. So warm to the touch; it smells so good. I'll clip some of the branches and bring them inside.

There's that laughter again. What are they doing?

Mary is calling, "Martha, come watch this puppy! Come for just a minute. Stop just a little while, and come look at him."

As I round the corner of our home to the garden, I can see a puppy leaping on Lazarus' legs.

The puppy is cute, but it better watch out for that bee. This is such a nice feeling—to laugh a little-- very nice!

Nevermind – I must get back to work; but Martha, Martha, you should breathe deeply more often.

"Mary, please come in and gather the mats for a quick shake. I want the house clean and fragrant for Jesus. He needs to rest. Come."

The last loaf is just about ready. The lentils are boiling, and the lamb is almost done.

"Lazarus! Come pull the lamb off the spit, please. Mary?"

What is that I hear? Footsteps coming up the walk? The time has come, and Jesus and his friends have arrived. They've made it to our home!

Mary and Lazarus are already out front. I need to get there to greet them.

"Jesus! Welcome friend, welcome! Come into our home and rest."

Oh! I've forgotten the wash basin! Where is Mary? Of course, there she is, already sitting at Jesus' feet.

Breathe, Martha, breathe! Why do I have to keep telling myself that? Ouch! My back! And where's the basin? There it is…and a cloth. The water, the pitchers of water. Where?

Oh, here they are. Now I can properly greet our guest.

"Jesus, come and wash the dust from your feet and rest."

He looks tired, as do his friends. It is good that they are here, and I wish I had the chance to sit and listen. Jesus always tells such profound stories. I'm sure there will be many conversations over the table in the coming weeks as Mary, Lazarus, and I try to figure out something Jesus tells us today. That's what I love about his visits. They last so long, at least in our minds and our hearts. He leaves us so much to ponder.

The lentils are boiling! If they had stayed on the fire a few more minutes, I am not sure what would have happened. I can't help but wonder where the platter for the lamb may be hiding.

"Lazarus, please carve up the lamb."

Setting the table, I can't help but enjoy the smell of the lentils and fresh herbs. Finally, Lazarus is coming with the platter of lamb. Jesus' friends' mouths are watering, I can tell—it's so wonderful!

Where is the yogurt? The mint? The salt and ....what else? The olives and dates, some nuts...Where are those almonds?

I hear chatter. What are they saying over there? Of course, Mary has planted herself, once again, right at Jesus' feet.

That really is making me angry. My shoulders ache, my back hurts, my fingers and arms are burning from the heat of the ovens. My hair is a mess. I'm so tired, so bone-tired, and I feel that I can't do any more! I won't do any more!

I hear the words come out of my mouth even before I have time to think about them: *"Jesus, do you not care that my sister has left me to do all the work by myself? Tell her then to help me."*

"Martha, Martha," Jesus pleads, *"You are worried and distracted by many things; there is need of only one thing. Mary has chosen the better part, which will not be taken away from her."*

Why is Jesus speaking to me in this way? How can he scold me so? I've done all of this for him! He looks so sad right now as he looks at me. What has made him so sad?

Breathe, breathe . . . He loves me. I know Jesus loves me. He loves all of us here—it's so plain on his face. What is it that I see in his eyes? Is it a question? It's as if he's asking me to trust him.

Yes. Yes, I can . . . I can trust him. I can sit and listen. And rest. Is that a smile I see on his face now? It's as if the closer I get to him, the more he smiles. It's a sweet, gentle smile.

Yes, Lord. You have my undivided attention.

The Martha and Mary in All of Us

Martha's and Mary's story is a timely, if not timeless, one. To read about Martha and Mary is one thing; to personalize it and see ourselves in the story—to walk in Martha's shoes—is another thing entirely. If we look deep enough, we will find that those shoes are quite familiar and familiar especially to caregivers. Just as Martha welcomed and served Jesus, caregivers welcome loved ones into their lives, serve them, and provide for their needs. Just as Martha felt frustrated with Mary, caregivers experience impatience, guilt, anger, and loneliness with loved ones and siblings. These side-effects are evident in Martha's life—it is right there in scripture, waiting for a pilgrim to journey deeper into the story and apply it to a hungry soul.

Ω

As we consider how their story—our story—intersects with our life on several levels, we must first understand what is going on with the historical background of the biblical text. Where are there points of contact, as well as the points of departure between the biblical world and our own? What is happening in this drama that we often overlook at first glance? How do these characters relate to us?

As the story above illustrates, we sense that Martha and Mary had a very close relationship with the One whom they called Lord, this Galilean peasant, Jesus of Nazareth. The author of this particular biblical story, Luke, picked up on this relationship and provided readers a glimpse into Jesus' private ministry with this incredible family. That the whole scene took place around a table reveals a distinct intimacy indeed; Jesus enters a sacred place in the home of these individuals.

Jesus' meeting with this family came at the middle of his public ministry. Earlier in his ministry, Jesus and his disciples served over 5,000 people with food (Luke 9:10-17). They were tired from caring for all of those people who needed Jesus the most. By the time readers get to Luke 10:37, we find him needing solace. What better place to rest than Martha and Mary's household, which was obviously a safe, caring place for God's Anointed One?

Martha was very concerned about Jesus' needs, and she did what was expected from many hostesses in her community. She readied her household, prepared a large meal, and provided care like any good caregiver in the first century would do. Like caregivers who feel obligated to care for their own loved ones, Martha felt obligated to prepare a meal fit for a king for her special guest.

Martha was quite productive in all that she did, but readers get the sense that if she took a break—even if only for a second—she might feel as though she failed Jesus as an effective caregiver. Martha was the doer. She was the task-oriented, older sibling who ensured that everyone else was well-cared for, and this left her utterly alone and frustrated. She wondered if anyone cared for her. She questioned Jesus' ability to understand her frustration, and she pointed out Mary's unwillingness to help in the household chores.

Yet, there is something deeper going on in this story. Although Martha became overwhelmed, she made a space for Jesus. She created a holy, sacred environment for Jesus, the Word of God, to rest. The interaction between Martha and Jesus has sacred value for caregivers today because Martha lived into her task—her calling or vocation—as one who cared for others.

Caregivers may connect with Mary as well. Luke wrote that Mary welcomed Jesus, but it was Mary who related to Jesus with attentive intimacy. Mary did not feel as obligated as Martha to meet the expectations placed upon her by society. Mary served Jesus, but she also took time to cherish a moment with Jesus in an atmosphere of sacred patience.

In fact, Mary related to Jesus in a way that was not characteristic of women in her day. Mary sat at the feet of Jesus, a posture reserved for male pupils who sought wisdom from teachers and mentors. This historical nuance allows us to realize that Luke intended to grab his audience's attention. He emphasized Mary's interaction with Jesus.

We, too, take pause when we read the story because we realize that the problem in this household was not necessarily related to what Mary was doing, but what she was not doing. Mary was not working, being productive, feeling pressured, or making use of her role as a caregiver—at least, not at the moment. Rather, she sat in silence in the presence of a Person who embodied God's intimate visitation upon the household. Mary valued rest in addition to hospitality, and she participated in a holy interaction. After all, if Jesus—God's very son— needed to rest after caring for so many people, then those who care for Jesus also needed to rest as well.

Martha observed Mary's posture and took note. Instead of taking advantage of this holy interaction with Mary and Jesus, Martha asked Jesus a difficult, accusatory, and confrontational question: "Don't you care?"

We cannot blame Martha for this harsh challenge. It is one question among countless others that caregivers ask in the midst of their frustrations. Martha cared for others; but who cared for her? She certainly felt that Mary had abandoned her. Caregivers care for others, but they often feel that no one cares for them.

Martha's challenge communicates several undercurrents going on in her spiritual life. First, Martha's question exposes an undercurrent of resentment. It is a type of resentment that comes when a caregiver cares for another person without taking the appropriate steps to care for her own needs. Martha's question stemmed from the burdens surrounding her role as caregiver. It stemmed from a Martha who was alone, exhausted, and restless. It came from a caregiver who did not have the resources, much less the time, to tend to her own needs.

The second spiritual undercurrent contends with guilt. There is a sense that if Martha stopped caring, then she would somehow fail Jesus. If she stopped, even for a moment, she would have faced the guilt that accompanied yet another unfinished task. Failure often leads to guilt, and guilt often threatens one's very being. It was an undercurrent that kept things in motion and threatened to suffocate Martha in the deep, murky tide of endless obligations.

Another spiritual undercurrent, one that is positive, is that of honesty. Martha was resentful indeed, but the fact that she asked Jesus this hard question shows a deep trust in Jesus. She trusted Jesus with her feelings. She asked a question that others might not have asked of God. Martha was courageous and honest, and she longed for Jesus to liberate her from her feelings of abandonment, guilt, and pain.

As these undercurrents threatened Martha and her hospitality, Jesus responded to her with a great deal of patience and sensitivity. He did not vilify her for being honest. He neither rebuked her nor denied that her feelings existed; rather, he broached Martha's resentment with love and care. That Jesus spoke her name twice emphasized Martha's status as a beloved child of God. In the person of Jesus Christ, God paid special attention to Martha and her concerns.

Jesus also reminded Martha that caregiving was not an end in itself and that caring for a loved one was not the only goal of hospitality. Instead, Martha's intentional care and concern revealed an opportunity for her to welcome God into her life and enjoy God's blessings. Martha's hospitality communicated great love for Jesus; however, Martha did not seem to realize that love was present in both the giving and the receiving of the caregiving relationship. Jesus modeled attentive sensitivity to

Martha by addressing her question; he expected her to do the same when it came to his teaching.

Blessings flow both ways. The caregiver is blessed by the act and the result of the caregiving relationship. The care receiver, oftentimes being unaware of it, gives blessings in return; blessings shared in quiet conversation, in companionable silence, in the squeeze of a hand, or an understanding smile. We see Jesus gently reaching out to Martha, hoping she will see the blessings for her as well as for Mary. Many times, He reaches for us when we care for others, and we are too resentful to recognize the divine interaction that takes place in our relationship with our loved ones.

Jesus did not blame Martha for her resentment; rather he affirmed her and sought to mend her relationship with Mary. Jesus pointed to Mary as a living illustration of one who provided care to a loved one while also taking the time to grow in the Spirit of the Lord. Mary provided bread for Jesus, and she also recognized that Jesus was the Bread of Life. Martha was so concerned about giving Jesus a delicious, nutritious meal that she overlooked the nutritious Presence that existed right before her very eyes.

Martha gave herself to a loved one as bread to be broken and served; but in failing to sit at Jesus' feet, Martha did not allow Jesus to be broken bread for her so that she could be made whole again. Mary, Jesus told Martha, chose a "good portion of bread"[5] when she chose to sit at Jesus' feet.

Ω

Now that we have made several points of contact with this story, what broader principles can we apply to caregivers? First, we must recognize that there is a little bit of Martha and Mary in all of us. The Martha in us is the task-oriented caregiver. It is the Martha in us who drones on about obligations and productivity resulting from the many tasks that lay before us, without which we would not feel very useful. The Martha in us feels that taking time to care for ourselves will lead to failure. Many caregivers already feel that they are not doing enough for their loved ones as it is. Accordingly, caregivers keep busy just to avoid facing the profound guilt that accompanies feelings of regret or failure. Like Martha, caregivers work endlessly in search of a false sense of value.

---

[5] The Greek word for "portion" refers to a measurement of food, particularly bread (and may be read as, "a portion of bread"). Also, the Greek uses the word *agathos*, or "good" to refer to this portion, which is more accurate than some translations of the verse, which posit that Mary chose a "better" portion of bread (see New Revised Standard Version). That Mary chose a "good" portion, not a "better" portion, does not support a history of interpretation that makes Mary better than Martha. That Mary chose a "good" portion (rather than "better") simply challenges Martha to choose between service and rest. Neither is qualitatively better, but one is more appropriate; thus, "good."

Mary exists in each one of us as well. God has placed the spirit of Mary in us to remind us that our true value comes from an identity grounded in a relationship with Jesus. Mary reminds us that we were created to be in communion with our Creator, a Creator who may not be all that impressed by the amount of work we do. Mary is the still small voice that creeps up in the midst of exhaustion. When we are at our rope's end, Mary reminds us that God is there to catch us. She lets us know that we are missing the intimacy needed to refresh our spirits. The Mary in us longs to sit at Jesus' feet and find a home in God's loving embrace.

There is also a temptation to think that Mary is somehow better than Martha. We long to be like Mary, and sometimes we come to hate the Martha in us because of the pressures that come with caregiving. This evaluation of Martha and Mary is natural. Throughout church history, many theologians have portrayed Martha as the *bad girl*. Both Martha and Mary, however, play important roles in this story. Martha provided much-needed hospitality at the expense of her own needs. Likewise, Mary was being a caregiver, but she also took time to sit at the feet of her Lord.

We should avoid choosing sides; rather, we must define the relationship between Martha and Mary as a partnership to a healthy, holistic spiritual life. Sometimes we are like Martha and give care to others; other times we follow Mary's example by resting in the presence of Jesus. Additionally, the biblical text challenges us to follow the command that Jesus gave to Martha. We can play both characters and balance our commitment to Jesus by setting aside time for work and time for spiritual practices.

The story also shows us that Martha had a profound resentment for the amount of work that she accomplished. She also had a great sense of loneliness in the midst of that work. Likewise, resentment is a thread that runs throughout the spiritual tapestry of caregivers. When we give that much time to others, we lose ourselves in the midst of our work. We are consumed by it, and we become angry with those for whom we care. We soon discover that we are also angry with God.

Resentment is a complex issue that requires honest reflection and prayer. Thank goodness that Martha gives us an example of a caregiver who shares her feelings with Jesus in honest dialogue. Caregivers are not alone in their resentment, and they too can feel free to express their deepest needs — no matter how confrontational — to Jesus.

There are many hindrances to honesty with God. Not many religious traditions encourage people to openly challenge God. For others, the idea of being angry towards God is uncomfortable. Too often, caregivers do not pray because they are afraid that they will offend God. The Bible — and Martha's conversation with Jesus in particular — shows us that honest prayer is an acceptable and appropriate part of our relationship with God. Honest prayer promotes intimacy and develops an open spirit in which one does not hide anything from an all-knowing Creator.

Another point of contact between Martha's story and that of caregivers is the loss of spiritual joy. This loss results from giving one's life in service to another and not taking the time necessary to re-fill his or her cup. A sense of joy—a deep spiritual joy— undergirds caregivers in some of the most grueling of tasks. We can imagine Martha waking up the day of Jesus' arrival excited, happy, looking as eagerly to his arrival as Mary. Over the course of the morning, as exhaustion sets in and resentment rears its ugly head, the joy diminishes. Martha exhausts her energy reserves and she has none with which to enjoy her company after all.

Yet, joy is what we find in the spiritual healing that can take place when we enter into an authentic conversation with God. As we find ways of sitting with our Lord and feasting on the Bread of Life, joy is the greatest blessing we can receive. It is only from an abundant life that we can serve others and maintain that type of joy. So, unless we take the time to sit and fill ourselves, we will often run short.

There is one last thing we encounter in this story. The entire drama takes place around a table complete with food and drink. Ironically, Jesus refers to food to describe one's spiritual life— Martha's many tasks *consumed* her, and they devoured who she was as an individual. Caregivers often lose their identity as independent people and serve up their very personhood as a meal for their loved ones to consume. In turn, care receivers will eat away at a caregiver's spirit until there is nothing left. This is especially true for caregivers who manage entire households in which they care for dependent loved ones and their immediate family, including children. These caregivers, often (and ironically!) called the "Sandwich Generation" in popular circles, are very busy; getting lost in the act of caregiving can consume them to the point of emotional and spiritual paralysis. These caregivers are "sandwiches" in more ways than one. Mary serves others, but she also takes time to eat of God's holy Bread of Life, Jesus.

The table scene in this story may remind us of the time when Jesus went to the wilderness to fast (Luke 4:1-13). After forty days, Jesus became very hungry and thirsty. Satan visited him at his most vulnerable moment and tempted him to turn stones into bread. The assumption was that Jesus did not need God to care for him; Jesus could very well take care of himself, thank you very much.

Instead of relying on his own miraculous power to turn stones into bread, however, Jesus turned the tide on Satan and said something profound: "People do not live on bread alone, but on God's every word" (Matt. 4:4). Jesus said this because he knew God called him to care for people who were hungry for God's salvation. Jesus, therefore, needed to rely on God's spiritual food as a primary source of meeting his own needs first. It was only out of that source of nourishment that Jesus entered his public ministry and served others.

Perhaps when she saw Jesus eat at her sister's table, Mary recognized that caregivers also don't live on bread alone. Jesus challenged Martha to choose him too, regardless of the quality and quantity of the tasks involved in caring for him. All of us must eat of God's Bread and move to a place of rest and self-care, of honesty with God and of restful, Sabbath peace, even if only for a few minutes each day or each week.

It is important to point out that Luke did not inform us as to whether Martha ever rested at the feet of her Master and feasted on God's Word. We can't help but think that this story plays out like one of those choose-your-own-adventure stories. If we pretend that we are Martha, then we must pretend that Jesus' challenge is for us. We must choose for her. Will we flounder like Martha and continue to let our obligations devour us, or will we take time to grow in the Lord and rest in his precious presence?

Ω

The process of balancing the Martha and Mary that exists in all of us requires us to become authentic and vulnerable in our spiritual lives. This is especially true if we feel like broken bread — broken and given to those for whom we care — and fail to feast on God's Bread. Without Jesus' help and without some sense of intentional spiritual discipline, the crumbs — our very life — will fall through the cracks of time, like sand running through a sieve. Are we going to allow Martha to overrun the kitchen of our soul, or are we going to make room in our spirit to allow both Martha and Mary to find an appropriate partnership while we minister to others?

In our hypercompetitive society—a society that promotes productivity, results, and a can-do attitude—Martha usually wins out every time, and this leaves us starving for spiritual energy and God's embrace. Spiritual hunger is not new for our times, and various faith traditions from across the globe reveal that humanity has hungered for spiritual vitality throughout history. Accordingly, a variety of spiritual practices elicit a *better way forward* in order to allow Martha and Mary to cooperate on our behalf. This *better way* consists of participating in spiritual practices that can be done either alone or in a community or small-group setting.

Ω

In order to assess how much we relate to Martha and Mary, we will introduce the discipline of journaling for our first spiritual practice. We recommend journaling because, of all the spiritual practices, it allows us to record our progress, feelings, and prayers over time. It also helps us understand that our spiritual journey unfolds as a narrative in which we find God at work. By committing to a discipline of journaling as the first order of business, we hope that our readers will see how much they grow in their relationship with God.

Journaling is a practice which one usually does in silence and solitude. Many times, it follows or precedes prayer and could contain aspects of confession, worship, celebration, and study (for further explanation of these and other spiritual practices, see Appendix A). Journaling is one way to open a door to spiritual awareness; and, oftentimes, amazing things happen as a result of articulating these God-movements in our life.

It often takes a special event or liturgical season, such as Advent or Lent, to motivate us to keep a journal. Other times, we start journaling when we discover that there are hardships in our spiritual lives. Indeed, our spiritual lives have seasons. Just as any journey contains periods of easy, straightforward travel, there are also times when crises and missed opportunities take their toll. We find ourselves living on a moment to moment basis; however, if we have developed our awareness of God's interaction in our lives, we will see where God uses certain moments to guide and direct us, to affirm or challenge us.

Sometimes, a season of our spiritual life is one that seems barren and silent. We wonder where God has gone. During a time of *winter* in our spiritual lives, if we take the time to journal, we can record the questions and demands we have of God, as well as the questions we have of ourselves. Winter can be a time of intense preparation, deep rest, and sometimes silent and unseen growth. Journaling is a good way of opening ourselves to the possibility that God's Holy Spirit is still at work deep within us even though we cannot sense God's presence.

A time of *spring* in our spiritual lives brings with it frequent insights, "aha" moments, and an increasing awareness of God's intentional, intimate connection with us. Of course, if there is a journal handy, remembering those insights and "aha" moments will be easier!   Those very special moments can carry us through the hot, dry *summer*. God gives sweet, tender food for thought, as well as time for considering those thoughts.

Spiritually speaking, an ⟨*autumn*⟩ in our journey with God is where all the fruit is harvested. We begin to revel in the deepening relationship we have established with God, and fruits of the Spirit abound.

As the seasons of our spiritual life continue, so the seasons of our physical life continue as well. If a friend or a loved one becomes ill and our time as a caregiver begins, we might scurry to write the overwhelming flood of feelings we experience when we are waiting for an important visit with a doctor to hear a diagnosis. Or perhaps our impatience inspires us to scrawl a short prayer while we wait to find out if we qualify for that mortgage or car loan, or when we are waiting to hear how far our loved one has moved through a terminal illness.

Each period of waiting and anticipation brings a unique set of emotions which includes doubt, faith, anxiety, confidence, joy, anger, frustration—you name it! Yes. . . name it. By taking the time to write down these thoughts and feelings, we take ownership of them.

The process of taking ownership of our feelings can open our eyes to see where that emotion is pointing. ⟨Anger⟩ can point to past hurts that were never resolved; ⟨frustration⟩ can point to old feelings of insufficiency or inadequacy. Such discovery can be difficult to accept, but our own actions and reactions are the only things we can control. If we discover something within ourselves that induces us to react in anger to certain circumstances, then would it not be healthier for us to deal with that root situation?

Digging out the tendrils of past frustrations, issues that need to be dealt with in forgiveness and compassion, is hard work. By journaling, we truly see God's presence in our lives, and we can experience the joy and release that are the natural results of this type of openness and introspection. We can prioritize, pray, and sift through a variety of emotions and questions. Over time, progress can be seen, habits clarified, and joys relived.

Ω

As an exercise in journaling, let us look back at Martha's morning and consider what she might have written in her journal that evening. First, utter a simple prayer to God for help. Second, put yourself in Martha's shoes, her heart, her mind, her tired body. Take a moment to slowly read the story at the beginning of this chapter again. Can you imagine how Martha felt? Can you hear the thoughts she might have been thinking?

Now, take a few minutes and write down those thoughts. Let them flow. As you write, remember that this is your journal, not something to be published. Do not get distracted by grammar or spelling issues if they arise. Get comfortable with using a pen, pencil, or keyboard to release your thoughts onto the page and write as freely as possible. If you notice that you are taking ownership of what you are writing, great! If not, remember that this is a spiritual *practice*, and sometimes practice is what is needed most. When you come to a comfortable stopping point, pull back and breathe deeply. Release and let go of what you have written. Allow your thoughts on the page to rest.

How did that feel? What emotions did the exercise bring up? Take a few minutes and write down your reflections on the process.

Oftentimes, it will take a week or two of committed practice to become comfortable with journaling, to find a style and a pace with which to record thoughts and feelings. Also, there are some who will not find journaling fulfilling at all. Others may find the idea of putting their inmost thoughts into words just too daunting. If that is the case, another way of recording thoughts is to use a scrapbook.

Cutting out images from magazines in order to represent one's thoughts and emotions can be just as effective. We can release many thoughts and emotions by simply gluing pictures into a book in a certain sequence or special arrangement. Another idea is to keep drawing supplies at hand and sketch out how you feel if you are more visual than verbal. Use air-dry modeling clay, available in re-sealable buckets, to express your feelings in a tactile manner. Be as creative and unique as you feel led to be, as long as you are able to review them for progress and insights at a later time. Remember: there are no rules.

As we continue to look at the story of Martha and Mary and how it relates to caregivers, make a habit of recording your reactions, those little things that touch you, and those God-enlightened moments that help you discover and feed on the Bread of Life.

Chapter One Study Questions

1. Do you practice spiritual hospitality? How and in what ways?

2. As a caregiver, are you feeling sustained in the way you practice spiritual hospitality? If not, what other spiritual practices do you engage in for sustenance?

3. What value judgments have you made about the way you practice spiritual hospitality? Why?

4. Have you been criticized for the way you practice spiritual hospitality?

5. Do you see room for change? Why or why not?

Chapter 2: Approaching God,
Unveiling the Spirit of Sabbath

Mary's Story

I live in a house of work, of non-stop activity! I live in a house that Jesus of Nazareth visits! My Spirit is so very excited at the thought of spending time with Jesus, listening to him speak of what is important in life, of pondering his words for days, sometimes weeks after he leaves. The love that pours out of him is palpable! My heart aches for time to just listen and take in what Jesus says, to spend time simply in his Presence, to be quiet.

Being quiet. That's always a challenge in our home. There never seems enough time to just stop and be still, just be. Our time to pray is so structured. Some days, I would spend all my time praying. I guess that isn't to be…especially today.

Ah, there's Martha. I guess I should stop staring off down the road and get busy. If I get busy, it won't seem like forever until Jesus comes.

"Yes, Martha. I will get the rugs and shake them. Of course, Lazarus and I will fill the water jugs."

Yet, if I had my way, I would simply wait. The Psalmists say that waiting on the Lord is good. The Lord! Yes…Jesus…is… what? The things he says always bring me to God, to thinking of what God wants of me, not what the world wants of me.

"Sorry, Martha. Yes, I will get busy!"

Now to find Lazarus and have him fill those water jugs. I wonder if Martha understands; if Martha ever ponders, deep in her soul, what Jesus brings. Martha is forever working; that's simply how she shows her love and concern for everyone in this house and those who visit. I wonder if Martha ever realizes I show my love by listening, by being still in wonder.

My, how wonderful everything smells. That's because of Martha! I must tell her. She cleans and cooks so mindfully. You can tell how much of her heart goes into it. The road is so dusty today, so no matter how well we sweep, more dust will come into the house. Of course, when Jesus and his friends come, it won't matter anymore. We will refresh and welcome them by washing their feet.

Ah yes. Jesus. How I long to sit at his feet and learn. His friends aren't too happy with me when I do that though. Yet, Jesus smiles at me when I do, a smile of encouragement and reward. My Spirit settles right down when I see that smile. My heart opens to hear, to receive what wisdom Jesus offers.

Duty calls. I must get busy and help Martha. Where is Lazarus? I hear him laughing…

Oh! Look at that puppy! I wonder where he belongs! Silly pup, chasing that bumble bee. He'd better watch out!

"Martha! Martha! Come see this silly puppy! Stop for just a moment, please."

Ahhh...it's so nice to see Martha laughing! Yes! So much gets said by a great laugh.

Yet, back to work! I'll set the table!

"Yes, Martha, I'll bring the platters; olives? Yes, I'll find them."

But wait, I see them! Jesus and his friends are coming down the road. Oh, what joy lifts my heart!

"Jesus! My lord! Welcome, come in and rest. All of you! Come, come in. Sit and relax. How was your journey?"

Of course, here's Martha with the basin and cloth; she looks so harried. I should have been more helpful today.

"Martha, I'll do this. Sit. Be still."

It is so marvelous to have Jesus in our home and Martha won't stop long enough to enjoy it. Why must everything be just so? Why must she stay so busy!?

"Martha, join me."

She is simply too distracted while I sit here at Jesus' feet with my heart so full as to be aching. This is the Presence I crave; I feel His words sinking deep into my soul, feeding my need for God's love and guidance.

What is Martha saying to Jesus?

"Lord, do you not care that my sister has left me to do all the work by myself? Tell her then to help me." But the Lord answered her, *"Martha, Martha, you are worried and distracted by many things; there is need of*

only one thing. Mary has chosen the better part, which will not be taken away from her."

The look on Martha's face is so sad. I cannot believe that Jesus has just rebuked her so. Yet, it seems that what he said to her is sinking in. Is she actually stopping? Is she actually sitting down? The joy I feel in my heart is beginning to show on Martha's face.

"Thank you, Jesus, for being here with us."

Finding Sabbath.

Shabbat, Sabbath, Sunday, Saturday; one hour or twelve or twenty-four — there is a diversity by which Christians understand God's rest. Yet, it matters very little of the title; what matters is whether you participate in it.

Sabbath is a way of being — and not just on the day you recognize to be your Sabbath. Sabbath is time spent away physically, emotionally, energetically, and spiritually. Sabbath is a time to be spent in the Presence of God, offering praise and thanksgiving for the abundance of God's provision, offering up our concerns and needs, offering up our hearts and souls for replenishment, refreshment: *re-creation*.

God's desire for us to stop and offer up our hearts and souls for replenishment, refreshment: *re-creation,* begins in Genesis when God rested! In the creation story, we hear God announcing each act of creation "good," finally stopping, and taking the day off: the seventh day. How often do we give ourselves credit as caregivers, as creators capable of acts of creation which are "good"? This review, this evaluation, needs to happen daily and can be a part of a daily time of Sabbath. Yet, just as God rested on the seventh day — whatever day of the week is considered Sabbath in your life, needs to be filled with rest.

Exodus 20:1-17 records the Ten Commandments. In 20:8-11, God gave a specific commandment regarding sabbath:

> *Remember the sabbath day, and keep it holy. Six days you shall labor and do all your work. But the seventh day is a sabbath to the Lord your God; you shall not do any work — you, your son or your daughter, your male or female slave, your livestock, or the alien resident in your towns. For in six days the Lord made heaven and earth, the sea, and all that is in them, but rested the seventh day; therefore the Lord blessed the sabbath day and consecrated it.*

"The Lord blessed the sabbath day and consecrated it." Consecrate: to make or declare sacred; set apart or dedicate to the service of a deity; to make (something) an object of honor or veneration; hallow; to devote or dedicate to some purpose. *So, to consecrate something means to set it apart and make it special.*

As caregivers, we find it extremely difficult to hold fast to that time away, that time to sit at Jesus' feet and listen to the Word. We find it almost impossible to have quiet time to ourselves in which to pray and take our cares and concerns, our joys and triumphs to God in prayer. However, it is only in this way, in this special, sacred time apart, that we can truly receive that which God so lovingly desires to provide us.

We must remember that Jesus needed time away from the crush of the crowds that began following him wherever he went, away from his disciples and their never-ending questions, and away from his family. Jesus would devote this time to prayer and intimate encounter with his Father. He knew this was the only way in which he could keep going, staying steadfast to his path.

Unfortunately, most caregivers are quite familiar with the cost involved in never stepping away from their work. Illness—physical and emotional—awaits a caregiver who never stops, never takes time to rest, to be re-created. Emotionally, caregivers are much more prone to depression and low self-esteem because of exhaustion. While in the throes of depression, caregivers can sometimes look at their lives, their care-receivers, *and God* with suspicion, resentment, and anger.

Even though those emotions seem to be aimed at the right person in the exhausted caregiver's mind, the suspicion, resentment, and anger are most often projected onto someone else, even God, because a caregiver simply cannot imagine being that angry and upset with himself or herself. Finding ways to reconnect with God, to the Holy, on a daily basis is an essential practice for caregivers. Sabbath happens when we stop and say *I am here, Lord*.

We assume that if a caregiver had a *Mary* mindset, finding time to reconnect would be easier, simpler. However, at times it is that very desire to be present to God that can engender frustration and resentment!

In the beginning paragraphs of this chapter, we hear those emotions creep into Mary's narrative. We hear it in Mary's questioning of Martha's *busyness*, just as we heard it in Martha's questioning of Mary's *stillness*. So, exactly how do the Mary and Martha in us all find time to sit with God? They do so through their intentions. Finding time with God each and every day is an essential habit, much like drinking enough water!

In fact, reconnecting with God could be as simple as drinking eight 8 oz. glasses of water a day. Thinking small but intentionally, each time a glass of water is poured and consumed, a prayer, an opening of one's heart could take place, an envisioning of God's grace pouring into one's heart, one's life—one's work.

There are many things we do each day without thinking. When accomplished with intent, they can become *rituals of invitation*. A ritual of invitation is a call to reconnect with God's presence in our lives for the day.

The way to reconnect on Monday, however, might be very different from Wednesday—and that would be okay! Other daily activities can be adapted and made rituals of invitation, including putting on lotion or moisturizer, making coffee, walking the dog, getting the paper, or cooking oatmeal. Daily activities involving opening something, slowly stirring something, or performing a repetitive or sequential action lend themselves most easily to ritual.

Rituals of invitation are ways of inviting God into our daily lives, intentionally, intimately, and conversationally. When God is invited, God always shows up! Learning to invite God into our lives and then recognizing God's presence begins an experience of Sabbath. In many Christian worship services, the service begins with a *call to worship* and a *prayer of invocation*. The congregants call each other to attend to the worship of God with *all of their hearts, minds, and Spirits*, and then they invoke God's presence. Rituals of invitation do the same thing for our personal lives.

Once we become creatures of habit in inviting God into our lives on a daily basis, then we can begin to acknowledge God's presence in our lives on a daily basis. At that point, the thought of taking a good chunk of time (which is a relative term) to sit in silence and pray becomes more feasible.

Taking time away — what a thought! Without a doubt, being a caregiver is a full-time job. Sometimes by including the one being cared for in our spiritual journey, we find avenues of growth appearing for ourselves and our care receiver. Prayers can be offered silently in the presence of a care receiver or, if comfortable, a caregiver offering prayers aloud can sometimes have a soothing effect.

Ω

> *Prayer is like a portable Sabbath, when we close our eyes for just a moment and let the mind rest in the heart. ... Traditional Sabbaths are filled with prayers. But we can begin slowly, with a simple prayer, like a pebble dropped into the middle of our day, rippling out over the surface of our life.*[6]

The spiritual practice we are going to introduce is a type of prayer called *centering prayer*. Centering prayer involves stilling the mind and opening the heart and soul in order to allow God to be present, to speak, and even to heal. In the practice of centering prayer, the use of *centering* or a "prayer word" is common to help the mind stay focused and free of distractions. Prayer words often include words such as *Jesus, Lord, Jesu, Peace, Love, Mercy, Christ have mercy*. Actually, any word which helps *you* focus and open yourself to God is appropriate. Also, in order to make sure you are free from concern, set a timer if necessary.

---

[6] Wayne Muller, *Sabbath: Finding Rest, Renewal, and Delight in Our Busy Lives* (Bantam, New York, 1999), p. 86.

Centering prayer can be simple:

1. Sit quietly with your eyes closed, hands held open. Simply rest for several minutes.

2. Say a short prayer to invite God to join you in your rest.

3. Trust that God is with you, and relax your body in response to that trust.

4. As your mind tends to wander, repeat your prayer word as a way to refocus your thoughts on God.

5. Do not concentrate on what to say to God; simply be with God.

6. End your time with God with a simple prayer of thanksgiving.

As you practice centering prayer, distracting thoughts are often present, especially when we are first beginning the prayer. What to do with them? There are various ways of clearing our heads: deep breathing, beginning the slow breath/word/breath rotation using one of the prayer words listed above; or, surprisingly, allowing those thoughts to float by unobstructed. The more attention paid to a thought as it occurs, the longer it takes to get rid of it!

Persistent distracting thoughts may point to areas of our life in which God wants to work. Consider writing them down to revisit them at a later time, allowing them to exist, yet "clearing" them from your mind. Journaling after prayer is also a great way to clear your mind of those pesky, monkey-brain thoughts!

With just a little practice and an investment of a few minutes per day, you too can find yourself sitting at Jesus' feet as attentive as Mary.

Chapter Two Study Questions

1.   Now that you have given thought to the differences between Martha's and Mary's spiritual hospitality, how will your own practice of hospitality change?

2.   Taking time to sit in silence is difficult for a caregiver. What distractions keep you from finding the time to sit and wait upon Jesus during your day?

Themes in the Dessert

Be Still + Know that I am God.

Chapter 3: Caregiving as Communion:
Broken, Whole, and Back Again.

Jesus' Story

He turned towards Jerusalem. Every step was that much closer to a fatal yet triumphant destiny, the shadow of the cross looming over his life and very soul. It was not a matter of years now, as it once had been when he worked in his father's shop. The time came when springtime erupted on the desert landscape and the Passover season ushered in renewed hope for God's redemption. He knew Jerusalem was ground zero; it was only a matter of time.

Jesus and his disciples spent the better part of the day walking to Bethany.

"Can you believe it?" Peter asked John, "We fed an entire crowd with only five loaves of bread and two fish" (Luke 9:10-17).

James spoke up from behind them, "Yeah, and did you see the look on that boy's face? The leftovers were more than enough to feed him and his family."

They laughed, and Jesus laughed too. Bread and fish. God always provided, and God would be there when Jesus needed God the most, too.

The talk of food made them hungry for lunch. It had been a full week of ministry. Aside from the miracle of feeding five thousand people, there had been the transfiguration of Jesus (Luke 9:28-36), an exorcism (Luke 9:49-50), a trip on the mission field (Luke 10:1-16), and a lawyer who asked Jesus about eternal life (Luke 10:25-37).

"Who is my neighbor?" the lawyer had asked.

"There once was a story about a guy who had been mugged on his way to the market..." Jesus responded.

It was a full and vibrant ministry, but now it was time to relax at the home of some old friends. Martha, Mary, and Lazarus had always been there for him. They had their issues, too, no doubt; but Jesus could always trust them to provide a safe place, a place for refreshment.

Not long after they saw the "Welcome to Bethany" sign, they came to their cozy destination. Mary was the first to greet Jesus. She welcomed him into the home. Lazarus shook his hand and took cloaks.

Jesus saw Martha when he entered the house. She was mixing a pot of lentils when he heard her yell from the kitchen, "Welcome, Jesus! It is so good to have you come today."

They washed up and gathered at the table. Mary served some drinks, but couldn't wait to sit down next to Jesus. Several disciples helped Lazarus break the bread that Martha pulled from the oven, its fresh scent filling the room.

Broken bread. It was hard for him not to think that the Romans and even his own Jewish brothers would break his body once he got to

Jerusalem. They would break him and consume him, not knowing that the very horrific act would make him the <u>Bread of Life for the entire world.</u> One loaf of bread, enough to provide for all of creation.

The victory of all of it — from the beginning to the end — overwhelmed Jesus. It was the single act of giving himself over to that fatal end that would fulfill a promise to make all who believed in him whole again in light of God's future glory.

"Man does not live on bread alone," Jesus once told his Adversary early in his ministry, "For we live on every word that comes out of the mouth of God" (Matt. 4:4). Jesus chuckled at the thought. How long had it been since he was in that wilderness?

Jesus couldn't resist the scent any longer. He took a bite of bread and started talking to Mary about God's Kingdom and the future that was in store for all of them. Martha finally came out of the kitchen.

"Jesus," Martha said, *"Do you not care that Mary has left me to do all of the work? Aren't you going to tell Mary to help me?"*

Jesus was taken aback. Did he care? Of course he did, but did she not realize that he was heading towards Jerusalem? Did she not consider that he was not going to be around much longer, and that his conversation with Mary — with all of them — was of utmost importance?

He took a deep breath and tried to calm Martha: *"Martha, Martha, you are concerned about so many things. You worry and are anxious."*

He looked at Mary. He looked at his hands fidgeting with the bread he just tasted. Its texture was soft, the crust firm. Broken bread. Then he looked back to Martha who still stood at the kitchen threshold with arms folded across her apron.

"There is need of only one thing," he continued, *"And Mary has chosen the good portion which will not be taken away from her."*

Martha stood silent now. The oven mitts gave her hands an enlarged, cartoonish look. Her hair was matted down from perspiration. She looked like broken bread too: shattered, given, consumed.

Jesus was right. Mary did choose the good portion, the very portion of bread that Jesus had made whole simply because He was God's very son. Man does not live by bread alone indeed. But Martha still stood there. Broken bread. At least, in that sense, she and Jesus had something in common.

Broken Bread

"I don't know who I am anymore," Alice, a caregiver to her grandfather, kept repeating. Her tears were wet against her cheeks, a balled Kleenex provided comfort in her hand. She explained that the moment she started caring for her grandfather was the moment she knew her life would be different.

It happened so suddenly. Alice's mother, who had cared for her as a single-parent, lost her battle to cancer eight months earlier and left her father — Alice's grandfather — all alone. Since Alice was an only child, she figured that her mother's caregiving role now fell in her lap. Grandpop (his name as long as Alice remembered) moved from Mother's house to Alice's within a week. That's when Alice realized that her life was not her own. Sure, he was independent enough for Alice to continue working, but he was unable to drive and needed supervision for his daily medication and eating regimen.

And his dementia seemed to get worse weekly. When Alice got home every evening, they lived in a routine of eating supper, cleaning up, and readying his medicine for the next day. She noticed that he asked the same questions repeatedly, and it was exhausting having to answer why he lived with her. He also asked how her mother had passed away. Every time she answered him and retold the story, she relived the nightmare.

Alice enjoyed work, but she quickly recognized that having any relationships outside of the home, whether with her girl friends or a romantic involvement with a partner, was going to be a challenge. She always wanted to marry, and she certainly wanted children. How was that going to be possible with Grandpop always home, always lingering and needing her attention?

He seemed to take the help she offered with little in return. He was a strong man, an independent man; but he offered little gratitude. He often pressured her with high demands and little patience. Also, the caregiver role was overwhelming, and she was not prepared to care for him so suddenly at her young age. Nor was she prepared to see Grandpop so vulnerable, like a child for which she was now responsible.

Caregiving and Grandpop required her attention, time, and money. He required companionship only she could offer (many of his friends were deceased) and attention when those barrage of questions came every evening. He did more than take her help; he—and the role she was forced to live into after her mother's death—consumed her.

By the time she met with her pastor, she was broken-hearted. She had forgotten who she was and what she wanted out of life. Her daily routine at work and home seemed monotonous. Sure, she had a purpose in caring for the man who had cared for her all of those years in her childhood, but the larger purpose of her life seemed to have died along with her mother.

"Who am I?" was a question born out of a crisis of self. Like a child figuring out who she is, Alice found herself in the dark night of the soul between who she was before her life as a caregiver, with all of her dreams and aspirations, and her life as caregiver, with all of the stress and responsibilities of caring for another person nearly three times her age. The question communicated a deep search for meaning in the midst of confusion and grief, as well as a search for what it meant to be caregiving in a contemporary context.

Ω

Alice is not alone in her crisis. Many caregivers sense a loss of self when they care for another person and devote their time to a care receiver. Many caregivers come to a breaking point when they finally realize it is time to rebuild a future in which successful and meaningful caregiving are integral parts of one's aspirations, hopes and dreams. "One of the risks of caregiving," writes theologian Brita Gill-Austern, "is losing one's life without ever finding it," and meaning is hard to come by.[7]

When Jesus sat at Martha and Mary's table, we can only imagine the various thoughts and emotions that might have gone through his head. As the above story implies, he might have thought of all of those occasions in which he broke bread in order to nourish all of those hungry souls for whom he cared on the way to Jerusalem. (He was a caregiver to the masses, and he never once hesitated to give himself away as one who made others whole again, liberating them to be fully alive in the presence of their God.)

By the time Jesus got to Martha's home, he anticipated having to make the ultimate sacrifice for the sake of those same people. In John 6, Jesus said that he was the "Bread of Life" (v. 35). During the

---

[7] Brita Gill-Austern, "Love Understood as Self-Sacrifice and Self-Denial: What Does It Do to Women?" in *Through the Eyes of Women: Insights for Pastoral Care*, ed. Jeanne Stevenson Moessner (Minneapolis: Fortress Press, 1996), p. 306.

Last Supper, Jesus pointed out that his body would be the "bread" broken for the entire world. The outpouring of his blood, furthermore, would provide the nourishing symbol of God's New Covenant with all humanity. This was a tall order; no wonder Jesus begged God to "let this cup pass" when he prayed at the Garden of Gethsemane before his arrest, trial and execution.

Alice and Jesus share a common narrative. And, like Jesus, caregivers sacrifice themselves in order to care for their loved ones. For many caregivers, this is a natural progression of the circle of life. Their loved ones cared for them; it is only natural to return the favor. For other caregivers like Alice, the role is thrust upon them prematurely, interrupting a life filled with hope of a future free from such burdensome responsibilities.

Yet, other caregivers choose willingly to care for their loved ones. A loved one could simply live with another relative or in a facility, but the caregiver cherishes the time together and makes accommodations for the care receiver to stay at the caregiver's home. Even in this situation, one in which plans and choices are intentional, a caregiver risks being consumed by the role in which he or she now participates.

There are many factors that motivate this drive to care for others, including family values, as well as larger societal mores. Even religious commitments can influence caregivers to serve others at the expense of taking time to care for themselves. Let us not forget, however, that Jesus did say that we can only love our neighbors as we love ourselves. We cannot love one another while neglecting our love in Christ.

Ω

Jesus certainly understood the larger sacrifice that had to take place in his own life in order to fulfill God's purpose, but Jesus never allowed the cross to define his entire destiny. It was the vision of the Risen Christ, the victorious One—the One who transfigured into a beacon of hope in the company of heroes of old—that informed Jesus' motivation and focus. Jesus' end was not the cross; rather, the cross was only a means to everlasting life and intimacy with God. It is the resurrection that defined Christ, and it is the resurrection—the finding of the new self baptized in the spirit of freedom, love, and dignity—that defines His followers.

Martha's dilemma envelops this truth: She let her *care* for Jesus define who she was. Both Jesus and Mary challenged Martha to gain a sense of identity by *whose* she was in relationship with her Lord rather than by *what* she did for her Lord. If a caregiver fails to care for herself and form the "who" in her life, as she grows in the Lord, then Alice's question, "Who am I?" will ring a hollow chord.

But to ask "Who am I?" can also beg the question, "Where am I to begin?" A possible way forward in figuring out who "I am" is to get to the root of the many conflicting feelings that war within every caregiver. Also, there is a need to express those feelings honestly and openly.

Many of these feelings and needs are attributes or characteristics with which caregivers wrestle but few try to resolve. The feelings all seem to be like shards of glass in a caregiver's life: to pick up any one piece or to handle even a few at a time runs the risk of hurting the caregiver.

What if Jesus took all of those glass shards that sit before us—in other words, broken bread—and puts them back together again so that they form a stained-glass window that allows God's light to shine through? What if this divine act enables us to become a beautiful icon in which others recognize God's compassion and love *in us*?

Consider how stained glass windows are constructed. They are not made from a single pane of glass; rather, an artist pulls together various colored shards and wraps them with a strong metal skeleton. Little pieces that seem to be randomly placed together interlock and form a larger picture. The window may depict a beautiful abstract shape, or it may take on the form of a picture, like a bird, or Jesus' baptism. No matter the subject, the point of a stained glass window is to let light become a new source of meaning for those who find themselves standing before it. The shards create a new reality for those searching for God's larger vision of the world.

As caregivers seek to serve others, it is critical to allow the light of God's love to reveal all of those unexpressed feelings and needs that have been neglected for so long. Although the risk of getting "cut" by those shards of glass will always remain, the hard work of stringing those strands together may garner a new reality that informs who a caregiver can *be* in Christ. God is the artist who offers us a larger vision of what those random shards may form. It is certainly true that a caregiver will not be able to return to the life that he or she had before a commitment was made to care for a loved one; but the new life that can come out of this meaning-making journey can lead to a magnificent rendering in which God's light provides ongoing strength, nourishment, and, ultimately, freedom from anger, fear, and guilt. Eventually, when resentment is expressed and guilt is cast off, the natural outpouring of forgiveness and grief work may ensue.

Ω

After Alice talked about her feelings related to caregiving, she admitted with some hesitation that she was in fact angry at her grandfather. She admitted that the situation, one that she was forced to follow, slowly ate away at her spirit and made her resentful. She realized that her anger was a result of grieving for the loss of her mother and her way of life.

As Alice discussed this, she immediately expressed guilt about her admission of resentment. "No one," she said, "wants to see a woman angry with her grandfather; people will see me as some crazy lady."

Alice talked about those feelings and admitted that she would be better off expressing them in a safe, confidential environment. After some encouragement, Alice finally overcame her fear that others were going to judge her for her feelings, and she was able to cry about the full range of emotions that existed inside of her. Such an outpouring of emotions also allowed her to express anger she felt towards God. She believed that He was the One who put her in this position in the first place.

After that, Alice celebrated the fact that she had the courage to admit that these feelings existed. Her tearful outburst and the safe environment gave her permission to "vent." She experienced a hint of freedom and a small taste of the holistic healing that God had in store for her. It was a miracle that eventually led to her "resurrection" as a caregiver empowered for ministry, unhindered by repressed emotions. She was bread broken, given, consumed; but, by working with the Lord, she allowed God to miraculously make her whole again.

Ω

Expressing our emotions to loved ones, trusted allies, and to God are important ways for caregivers to improve their emotional and spiritual well-being. Many caregivers find it difficult to be honest, especially with God. Some caregivers, for instance, have grown up in a religious tradition that forbids being honest with God with all the emotions that one feels, like anger or hurt. Other caregivers do not know how to pray and do not know what words to use in prayer. Prayer can seem like wasted words or, worse, a soliloquy that goes unheard and unanswered when caregivers are uncertain how to pray.

Recognizing this need in humans, God saw to it to include a prayer book in the Bible, the book of the psalms. The psalms, all 150, include a diversity of prayers and express a wide range of emotions. The psalms speak to various settings and have many functions.

There are psalms that are prayers by individuals, and there are psalms that instruct the entire community how to pray. There are psalms that express joy and others pain. There is a psalm for every type of prayer.

When words fail us or we forget how to pray because of the depth of our grief, guilt, or hardship, the psalms can provide words and a template to restore our relationship with God. They help us become vulnerable to God, and they remind us of who God is and of God's steadfast love and faithfulness.

The spiritual practice for this chapter is to pray a psalm. In order to follow through on the theme of coming to God as one "broken" and poured out for others, we chose Psalm 69 as an appropriate prayer for caregivers who may be in the midst of crisis and suffering.

Psalm 69 is accredited to David, who was Israel's king during the "golden age" of the small nation at the turn of tenth century BCE. Whether

David penned this psalm before he was king, while on the run from his murderous predecessor, King Saul, or while he was king under siege from hostile neighbors cannot be determined. What can be determined is that the psalm was an individual prayer likely set to music. Psalm 69 sought to inspire God's people in a time of distress, a people who were in a position of disorientation and anxiety.

After you read through the entirety of Psalm 69 in the Bible translation of your choice, you may recognize that the psalm is made up of three general parts: Verses 1 - 12 is the part of the prayer that lets God know how the author feels.

- "I sink deep into the mire...I have come into deep waters" (v. 2).

- "I am weary with my crying...my eyes grow dim" (v. 3).

- "I have become a stranger among my kin" (v. 8).

- "I am the subject of gossip" (v. 12).

Note also that there are external factors causing distress:

- "Many are those who would destroy me" (v. 4).

- The psalter was the focus of insult (v. 10) and gossip (v. 11, 12).

Verse 13 is a transitional verse in the psalm because the author moved from emotion to acknowledgement that God can answer prayer: "My prayer is to you, O Lord. At an acceptable time, O God, in the abundance of your steadfast love, answer me."

This appeal begins the second half of the psalm (v. 13-28), which includes a range of specific requests made to God. It is what scholars call the _petition_:

- "Rescue me" (v. 14).

- "Do not let the flood sweep over me" (v. 15).

- "Answer me" (v. 16).

- "Do not hide your face" (v. 17).

- "Draw near to me" (18).

Like the first part of the psalm, the second part interweaves individual, personal appeals in prayer and appeals to exact justice on external influences of hardship (esp. v. 22-28). It becomes clear at this point in the psalm that this lament, like many other psalms of lament, resulted from a dire situation in which the psalter (or God's people whom the psalter represented) had a conflict with others. There is a possibility that this scorn was born out of the psalter's enthusiastic care—and caregiving!—of God's temple (v. 9-12).

And the honesty! This prayer does not go easy on the psalter's enemies: He wishes God to "let their table become a snare" (v. 22) and "let their eyes be darkened" (v. 23). He begs God to make their camp a "desolation" and to blot them out "of the book of the living" (v. 28). We would feel so guilty if our prayers held such venom; and although we would never wish death upon our enemies, this prayer is a school of honest vulnerability before God.

For caregivers today, this point is important because a number of external circumstances can be considered "enemies" that force the caregiver to pray a lament. The caregiver role itself can become a source of conflict that has laid a "snare" for God's beloved (v. 22). In other situations, siblings or family who "scorn" the caregiver can add undue stress in the caregiver relationship. "I looked . . . for comforters," the psalter prayed, "but found none" (v. 20).

The psalm does not encourage vigilantism or vengeance, but it does encourage honesty: It challenges us to "get out" all that we keep inside of us, be it despair, resentment, or joy. By the second part of the psalm, readers can tell that all three sentiments are included in this ancient author's beautiful poetry.

The third part of the psalm (v. 29-36) concludes with words of praise to God. This records the author's movement from despair to hope, from passive suffering to proactive celebration. It moves from individual praise--"I will praise the name of God with song" (v. 30)—to an invitation for the entire community to praise God: "Let heaven and earth praise him...For God will save Zion" (v. 34, 35). Now that we see the beauty and pattern of Psalm 69, we can move into how to pray the psalms.

Ω

Praying the psalms is an important part of growing one's spiritual life. The psalms give voice to our prayers. They are a school of honesty. The psalms slow us down and acknowledge that there is a time for mourning and complaint as well as rejoicing and praise. At times, there are moments of anger and a call for vengeance.

Perhaps we fail to see these movements inherent in the psalm because we tend to read the psalms too quickly. Ours is a prose culture not familiar with the slow, methodic pilgrimage poetry requires of each reader.

There is a good chance, however, that each psalm—Psalm 69 especially—was a work of art crafted over many hours if not days. No wonder the author can move from peril to praise, changing the tone of voice and giving words that express grief, anger, and hope all in the same poem. Additionally, the psalm was meant to be sung or recited as song, not necessarily read in the quietness of one's study or private devotion. Nevertheless, the author's melodic and intentional "slow" method of writing obliges us to invoke a slow method of reading and, if possible, reciting.

We need not skim over the words or read it as we read a book or newspaper column. It is more appropriate to live into the words, letting each word, phrase, scripture, or section speak to us in particular ways. "Oh, how I love your law!" exclaims the author of Psalm 119, "It is my meditation all day long" (v. 97). Living into the words is a form of meditation in which we allow God's words to become our words, the author's honest words to become the honest utterances of our yearning to be honest with God.

One method to help us live into the words of the psalms is to read them aloud. This helps us form the words in our mouth, connect God's scripture with our heart, and soften our ears to what the Spirit may want us to hear. For a caregiver in the depths of grief and despair, repeating Psalm 69:2 aloud may be helpful: "I sink in the deep mire, where there is no foothold." The graphic poetry brings tears to the eyes and helps us to see our distance from the surface ("the deep mire") where we can breathe in God's steadfast love. A caregiver can then move through the psalm and rest in verse 14: "Rescue me from sinking in the mire; let me be delivered from my enemies and from the deep waters."

A prayer unanswered can veer into verses 16 and 17a: "Answer me, O Lord, for your steadfast love is good; according to your abundant mercy, turn to me. Do not hide your face!"

Although silence and God's hidden majesty may remind us that answers to our prayers are sometimes elusive and can come when we least expect it, we can end prayer with anticipation that God will indeed hear us and answer our prayers in due time: "I will praise the name of God with a song; I will magnify him with thanksgiving."

In conclusion of praying through the psalm and allowing some of it to connect deep within our heart, soul, and mind, it may be appropriate to rest in silence and let the psalm brood. It is in silence that the Spirit has room to speak back to us; it is in silence that a caregiver may take note of any part of the psalm that continues to resonate and stand out. As instructed before, journaling is a wonderful way to make the psalm a caregiver's own. If a word or scripture stands out, this is the time to record it along with any feelings or commentary that the caregiver deems appropriate. The caregiver may also record how it felt to pray through a psalm that forces her to be honest with any grief or anger that may exist. End the time with the humble words of another psalm, Psalm 19: "Let the words of my mouth and the meditation of my heart be acceptable to you, O Lord, my rock and my redeemer" (v. 14).

Chapter Three Study Questions

1. Are there any areas of resentment in your life?

2. What makes you angry about caregiving?

3. What steps do you need to take in order to bring anger and/or resentment before God in prayer?

4. What Psalm appeals to you in your own prayer life?

Chapter 4: Back to the Altar –
A Life of Worship

"But the Lord answered her, 'Martha, Martha, you are worried and distracted by many things; there is need of only one thing. Mary has chosen the better part, which will not be taken away from her.'"

There is need of only one thing. What would it feel like to stop? What would it feel like to forgive ourselves of our mistakes, for all the things that didn't get accomplished in our day of caregiving?

There is need of only one thing. What a profound statement. Do you believe it? As a caregiver, it is essential to find a way of forgiving and loving ourselves, those for whom we are caring, and those around us who question our every decision. Forgiving and loving in this way enables us to approach the Altar of our lives and truly enter a life of worship.

What is so needful about a life of worship? Life lived with a worshipful heart opens us to the times of *Mary,* to the times of deep joy and happiness as we take our place at the feet of Jesus. At times those opportunities are fleeting and thus must be recognized and taken at a moment's notice. At times those opportunities are bounteous and full and extended.

Each of these opportunities presents times where caregivers can stop and listen, listen to how

God is speaking into their lives. *These opportunities are times of worship*.

Ω

Don Saliers, in *Worship and Spirituality*, says that worship is about *remembering*. Not simply recalling acts of old, but a re-member-ing—*a rejoining of those acts of old*. By rejoining those acts of old, we actually bring them into the present. What acts of old would those be? *The unconditional love offered and proved by the life, death, and resurrection of Jesus*. As we move through our days of caregiving, there are opportunities—brief or extended—in which we are asked to (re-member) that love and offer it to ourselves, to those of whom we are taking care, as well as to others we have in our lives. *Those opportunities are worship*.

Worship is a time when we stop and listen. Worship begins by being aware of God's Presence, then offering praise and thanksgiving. We ask for God's forgiveness for the ways in which we have separated ourselves from God and from others. As we have moved through awareness, praise, thanksgiving, and confession, we end by rejoicing in knowing God's love and forgiveness are ours—to keep *and* to share.

How does this relate to a life of 24-7 caregiving? How does a caregiver who is bound to the house, caring for a loved one with dementia or for someone who is bed-ridden, find time for worship? When involved in a life of caregiving, our expectations and experiences of worship change. Rarely are we involved in communal worship as we have come to understand it. The experience of communal worship found in a church building with our *community of faith* gathered around us becomes more difficult. Perhaps, caregiving as a life of worship can begin to build a new *community of faith*.

Building a life of worshipful caregiving begins with our own relationship with God and encompasses those around us and their relationships with God. Beginning with our own relationship with God provides ritual and sustenance to begin the day! Asking God's help in being aware of God's Presence throughout the day, most especially as the day starts, sets the tone for the worship that the next 24 hours will present.

[handwritten margin note: First Thing in AM]

As we become more aware of God's Presence, we will begin to notice more freely the acts and words which bring praise to our heart. Small things that perhaps usually go unnoticed will begin to radiate God's love. A loving smile on the face, a gentle hug, a hummed song – all of those are ways of offering God praise and thanksgiving for an enduring, steadfastly faithful presence.

Another aspect to being more aware of God's Presence is that of confession. Yep! We all do things we regret later – especially in the stressful and time-pressed days of a caregiver. Instead of allowing these things, most often smaller in nature, to mount up in the heart, confess them. Ask for God's forgiveness and a reassurance of God's unconditional love and understanding. Grace begins to pour in when we have developed our awareness of God's Presence, when we offer up praise and thanksgiving, and when we are willing to confess our shortcomings and receive, *willingly*, God's forgiveness and love.

Willingly? Have you ever said, "I'm sorry" to someone and received forgiveness, yet did not truly receive that forgiveness because you did not take it into your heart? It's the same way with God's forgiveness of our wrongs.

There is simply no way God can work within us to make our wrongs right unless we receive God's forgiveness truly and take it into our heart. Receiving forgiveness means letting go of what we have done and releasing all of the guilt and shame surrounding the act which needed forgiveness in the first place. Once done, forgiveness can heal our wounds, can brighten our outlook, and can positively influence our relationships going forward.

Ω

Creating our days to be days full of worshipful caregiving is a wonderful way of setting the tone in our own hearts and in the hearts of those around us to give and receive forgiveness. Not flippantly—no—but quite sincerely. Give and receive forgiveness when the wrong is fresh and not given time to fester.

Perhaps our new community of faith will look different than those who used to sit next to us in the pews on Sunday morning. Yet, who will they be? A word here about the term community of faith: As this term is used in this chapter, a community of faith is a group of people willing to support each other spiritually — not religiously — the difference being one of respecting each other's spiritual journey without sweating the details of denominational backgrounds.

The first members of this new community of faith will, of course, be you and your care receiver. If your care receiver is a family member, then you will most likely have a sense of his or her spirituality; however, sometimes perhaps not. In any event, gentle conversations about God and the Spirit's presence in a given situation can open hearts and minds to consider different outcomes, different angles to getting through a hard patch. **This is worship.**

Other members of this new community of faith can be neighbors, friends from church or school, colleagues from work. When our awareness of God's presence in our lives is awakened or increased, sometimes our relationships change. The difference in our relationships is oftentimes based in a sense of wonder or curiosity about the other person's spirituality. **This is worship.**

Are you and your care receiver on a prayer list? If so, all of those prayer warriors are a part of your new-found community of faith. **This is worship.**

Will you and your community of faith ever see each other all together in one place? Perhaps, perhaps not. If you are comfortable having people in your home under your particular circumstances, then invite them! If not, having one person over at a time here and there for spiritual conversation and friendship will suffice. **This is worship.**

The focus of thinking in terms of a community of faith is community. How you can make that community become a reality depends upon your specific situation.

Ω

Your new community of faith looks different and acts different than the typical go-to-church-every-Sunday community of faith. What is your part in it? How do you connect with it? Over the next few pages, we will offer for your consideration many ways in which you, as a caregiver, can develop a worshipful life, a life that feeds and sustains you and those for whom you care. Rest assured that we are aware of just how busy a caregiver's day is; so, as you read and consider the following ideas, know that you are encouraged to pick and choose what works best.

Romans 12:5 speaks of the Body of Christ as being one body with many members in which each member serves an important and good purpose. The way we go about being the Body of Christ day in and day out is how we serve: in our caregiving we serve, in our families we serve, in our jobs outside of caregiving we serve. Yet, how do we get fed and sustained in this service?

We begin each morning by inviting God into our day, asking Christ to walk with us in each and every experience we work through during our day.

74

Do you have time to add one more thing, one more activity—no matter how holy—into your morning rituals? Rituals. Yes, that is the key. What sort of activities do you do each and every morning, without fail? Open a cabinet? Get coffee started? Pour yourself a cup? Put on moisturizer and make-up? Shower? Read the newspaper? Take the dog for a walk?

With each activity you do without fail, you can develop a ritual of invitation. Daphne's favorite is one she does as she moisturizes her face:

> *I look in the mirror and do my best to see the face of God looking back at me. As I touch my forehead with lotion, I ask God to direct my thoughts. As I touch my eyes, I ask God to be my vision. As I move on to my lips, I ask that God put the words in my mouth. As I add lotion to my throat, I ask that God put a song in my throat to sing God's praises throughout the day.*

Do you have a workout routine you move through each morning? Yoga? Tai chi? Body prayers are another way of waking up and plugging into the Body of Christ.

> *I enjoy the Chalice Prayer. To experience it, stand with your feet shoulder-width apart. Put the palms of your hands together as in prayer in front of your heart and center your thoughts. Pushing your palms together, raise your arms over your*

head, opening out to form a chalice. Receive what God has to give you. Bring your arms down and around to the front and hug all that God has given you close to your heart. Now, stretch out your arms in front of you in a gesture of offering. Offer what God has given you to the world. Typically, I move through this prayer three times, taking my time, not rushing any aspect of it.

Wow! Now you are awake and tuned in to the Presence of God, having invited God into your day. **This is a Call to Worship.**

What's next? Staying awake and tuned in! We all know that sleep is sometimes an issue for caregivers. Having a body prayer that you enjoy and can do wherever you find yourself will help keep blood flowing to your head and your heart, making all of those decisions needing to be made more easily and with better clarity. *Having an activity during the day to reconnect your body, mind, and Spirit is worship!*

If your care-receiver is physically capable of sharing in this experience, teach them, and share with them this simple, holistic way of approaching God. *You are then connecting with your community of faith.*

Another opportunity for worship arises when there is a time of silence. Sometimes in the day of a caregiver, time to read opens up while the care receiver is napping or otherwise engaged. Having something on hand to read that you find uplifting is important. No one can really tell you what that might be. Of course, scripture is always a doorway to hearing God's word for our lives. Lighthearted books and books about any number of non-religious or spiritual topics can also serve as catalysts to hear God's voice. How can that be?

Have you ever read something unrelated in any obvious sort of way to things spiritual — such as an historical novel or a science fiction story — and find yourself inspired to think deeply about the meaning of something to your Spirit, to the world? Ever had a word jump off the page and start a cascade of thoughts taking you deeper and deeper? Such an experience is a taste of spiritual reading. Spiritual reading is reading for inspiration, not so much for information. God can use anything we read to make us think and draw closer to the Holy Spirit!

When we intentionally choose to spiritually read a text, we set out reading slowly, intentionally open to receive what God chooses to give us. When a word or phrase radiates meaning, stop and take a few moments to consider it. Write down your thoughts in your journal. You can either leave the text you are reading and spend time journaling or make a note and return to the reading. It is an amazing process to hear God's voice in words so familiar! **This is worship!**

The same thing can occur when singing along with the radio or a favorite hymn! What is God doing? What is God trying to give you? Most of us have a favorite soothing song, a favorite make-me-happy song—I call it Whistle While You Work: Singing Songs of the Heart. Even when we hum or simply sing a song in our heads, our moods change, we smile more, our hearts are lifted. During worship in a church service, the reason we sing is to lift our praise to God, our thanksgiving for all that God has given us. We sing to lift our worries and concerns to God for God's healing and comforting solace. In our lives as caregivers, leading a worshipful life includes this singing—this lifting of our hearts in praise and prayer. Why not sing a song of our heart? **This is worship!**

Does your care receiver have a favorite song? Do you play the piano or another instrument? Perhaps music can be an avenue, a connection to worship for those for whom you care. For people living with dementia, music is a miracle! Music is stored in an area of the brain that remains relatively unaffected by dementia. Music can be comforting and soothing or even stimulating! Consider Psalm 150:3-6:

> *Praise God with trumpet sound; praise God with lute and harp! Praise God with tambourine and dance; praise God with strings and pipe! Praise God with clanging cymbals; praise God with loud clashing cymbals! Let everything that breathes praise the Lord! Praise the Lord!*

This is worship!

Ω

There is yet another aspect to living a worshipful life—times of quiet reflection. This includes time spent in silence and stillness waiting upon God, listening to the prayers of God within us (Romans 8:26), listening to the gentle words God gives us in the midst of worship. Finding the time for quiet reflection can be a challenge. However, as you begin shaping a worshipful life for you and your care-receiver, your day will change. Perhaps the change will be in attitude. Perhaps the change will be in how hurried the day is. Perhaps the change will be in how often quietness is noticed, a space to breathe opens up.

When that space opens up, take the opportunity to stop. There is need of only one thing. All of the preparation, the invitation, the prayer, the singing – **all of the worship you have allowed to happen** throughout the day culminates in this space, in this special time to stop and listen. There is need of only one thing. Will you allow yourself to become Mary? To sit at Jesus' feet—however briefly—and listen to the marvelous, compassionate, loving things He has to say?

Let us have one last look at worship and your community of faith. We mentioned earlier in this chapter that neighbors, colleagues, or members from your church may fill in the membership of your new community of faith. You might find that there is someone in this new community is special and understands more deeply where you are in your journey. That individual could become a trusted spiritual friend. As you seek to grow in your faith and closer to Christ, you will find that having a companion on that journey is helpful.

The relationship of spiritual friendship is different from a simple friendship with a neighbor. A spiritual friend is someone with whom you spend time listening to God and to one another with love and respect.

Time with a spiritual friend is not a time for fixing anything. Nor is it a time to give or receive advice. Rather, it is time spent seeking the face of God in the face of our friend as well as in ourselves. Each person has an opportunity to share where they are, or how their day went with respect to an awareness of God's presence and interaction. What is shared is simply received, without comment. Gentle questions can be asked to make sure the speaker has said all that needs to be said. Ending such a time together with prayers for each other – either silently or out loud — brings a fuller sense of worship to the time. **This is worship**.

Chapter Four Study Questions

1. How do you define worship?

2. In what ways do you experience worship?

3. How can you adopt or adapt your ideas of worship into your caregiving?

4. How does your faith tradition inform your experience of worship? How does it hinder your experience of worship?

Chapter 5: Called to Care

A Caregiver's Story

Luanne is a caregiver for her mother, Frances. She is one of nearly 20 million caregivers caring for an aging parent; and, like many of them, Luanne feels a great sense of obligation and joy to care for the person who once cared for her.

"Taking care of my mother is what I'm supposed to be doing in my life, this is where God has placed me," Luanne mused. Luanne talks as if she has been called to care, as if she is simply responding to the divine purpose that God has set before her in this late season of life. Luanne talks as if she has been thrust into a larger-than-life plan that connects her caregiver role with the grand scheme of God's redemptive history. Despite the guilt and frustration that Luanne often feels, her role as caregiver is profoundly sacred and satisfying.

Luanne's feeling of participating in a divine imperative is not unique. In one study of 40 caregivers, researchers found that a major motive for providing care to families was born out of the caregivers' response to a meaningful "call" upon their lives.[8]

Another caregiver, Cybil, even saw her role as caregiver as something that usurped other priorities

[8] Nancy Guberman, Pierre Maheu, and Chantal Maille, "Women as Family Caregivers: Why Do They Care?" *The Gerontologist* 32:5 (October 1992): 610.

in her life: "God never planned for me to get married. He knew I'd be the primary caregiver [of my parent], and it is what God planned for me, so I do it."

Ω

Throughout this book, there has been a discussion on self-care. The assumption is that caregivers do not take enough time to rest, reflect, and meditate on the important spiritual practices that create a healthy caregiving environment. The movement of a healthy spirituality, however, always turns from the inward practices—such as prayer and silence—to the outward-focused vocation of engaging in meaningful ministry. In this case, that ministry is caregiving. Whether a caregiver is forced into that position does not negate the fact that caregiving, in whatever form, can provide a sense of mission and become a powerful catalyst for the ministerial vocation.

Vocation: The utter mention of the word implies something sacred and holy. In the Catholic tradition, vocation refers to the priesthood. The idea of vocation in the Protestant church also points to something entirely devoted to Christ's Church or to the sacred realm of professional ordination. According to the Bible, however, vocation has a broad, nuanced meaning.

A vocation can be a calling from God, a response to God, or a commitment to live life as one on mission for God. In the words of Gary Badcock,

"The Christian calling refers to the reorientation of human life to God through repentance, faith, and obedience; to participation in God's saving purpose in history; and to the heavenly goal: 'I press on toward the goal for the prize of the heavenly call of God in Jesus Christ' (Phil 3:14)."[9] Martin Luther, the famous German church reformer of old, gives us a simpler understanding of vocation. He saw vocation as a calling to join God in meeting the needs of one's neighbors. A vocation does not reach up to God, so much as it "bends" a person "down toward the world."[10]

Caregiving is a vocation because it is a way to live out God's *agape* love in the world and serve the needs of others. *Agape* is Greek for unconditional love. Unlike other uses of love in the Bible, such as *phileo* (friendship) or *eros* (romantic) love, *agape* love seeks nothing in return. It loves simply for love's sake. This can be a powerful and meaningful way to improve the caregiving role and help caregivers cope with the stress of caring for others, especially caregivers who are in difficult circumstances.

A problem comes, however, when a caregiver sees vocation as a burden rather than a blessing. Sometimes caregiving can force a caregiver to sacrifice much-needed life or economic goals. This is

---

[9] Gary Badcock, *The Way of Life: A Theology of Christian Vocation* (Grand Rapids: Wm. B. Eerdmans, 1998), 3.

[10] Gustaf Wingren, *Luther on Vocation*, trans. by Carl C. Rasmussen (Philadelphia: Muhlenberg Press, 1957), 10.

especially true for women caregivers because society places the added expectation upon women that they must care for entire families, including extended family at times—and to do so without complaint! Luther may be to blame here: While insisting that Christians see their duty to neighbors as a vocation, he also promoted humility and sacrifice even at the expense of personal comfort and health. Melanie May, in an honest evaluation of this assumption of vocation, writes:

> *We have been socialized to do our duty, not to follow our desire. Any other course of action would be wanton – selfishness, sinful. And so, as a woman, I have wrestled with vocation. I have struggled to trust and to value my own inner authority. I have been fearfully taught not to trust and value my own inner voice, but instead to attend to the duties and the expectation and orders and patterns and 'shoulds' defined for me 'out there.'*[11]

By living in light of Jesus' own vocation of dying on the cross, caregivers often die on the cross of self-sacrifice to the detriment of receiving much-needed care and solace for a meaningful vocation in the first place. Suffering for the sake of Christ is taken out of its biblical context and used as a masochistic tool that oppresses caregivers to the point of dis-ease and unrealistic self-denial.[12]

---

[11] Melanie May, "One Woman's Wrestling with Vocation" *Brethren Life and Thought* 46 (March 2004): 234.

A closer look at the Bible informs us that we are to live out our calling as something sacred, while at the same time balancing love for others with love of self. After all, Jesus did say that we need to love others as we love ourselves, not at the expense of ourselves.

Ω

A good place to start in exploring a well-rounded sense of biblical vocation is in the book of Isaiah. In chapter 6 (vv. 1-8), the prophet Isaiah experienced a vision of the very throne room of God. He was overcome with awe as he looked upon "the Lord sitting on a throne, high and lofty." Mythical beings with six wings surrounded God and Isaiah, and they sang a song declaring God's holiness.

At once the room filled with smoke, and that's when Isaiah came to his senses. Isaiah realized that he had just looked upon God, something no mortal had ever done, and he immediately recognized his own lack of worth: "Woe is me! I am lost, for I am a man of unclean lips" (6:5). How else does one respond—prophet or not—when there is such an intimate and powerful encounter with the Creator of the cosmos?

One of the angelic beings flew to Isaiah and purified the prophet's lips with a burning ember. This act of purification extinguished Isaiah's guilt and freed him up to speak God's Word and live into

[12] Gill-Austern, 308.

a vocation tailor-made for him. When God asked who God might send to Israel to bring Israel back in relationship with the Creator, Isaiah confidently responded with the bold announcement: "Here am I; send me!"

A little research into this text sheds light on this powerful experience. Isaiah's vision came at an uncertain time in the life of his homeland, Judah (the southern region of modern-day Israel). Several neighboring empires sought to overthrow the little nation, causing Judah to build an alliance with Assyria. By the time Judah's king died, Assyria was taking advantage of this alliance and exploiting Judah for much-needed resources.

Second Kings 15:1-7 tells readers that Uzziah was a good king, one favored by God. Uzziah managed this alliance well but failed in removing the "high places" in Judah that threatened to usurp God's power and temple in Jerusalem. These "high places" were a testament that not everyone in Judah believed that Israel's God was the only God. These high places were used in worshiping other gods.

We are a people with "high places" as well, distractions that get in the way of our relationship with God. These distractions can be something as innocuous as the technology we use (how often do we spend more time on Facebook than in prayer?) or as life-transforming as our careers. No matter the distraction, there are things in our life that can get in the way of our devotion to God, and when God comes near to us, we can't help but repeat Isaiah's words: "Woe is me!"

Our high places exist in our life precisely because we think that we have to out-perform God. Instead of seeing God's calling as a gift to be shared, we see it as yet another burden that only leads to failure. We do not necessarily fail in reality, but in the recesses of our mind, we assume that we cannot please God and fall short. We create high places as alternative places to worship, because worshipping a God who has too many expectations of us is just too hard to bear. The guilt is overwhelming, and our vocation becomes something from which to escape rather than live into. We are filled with woe not because God does have unrealistic expectations, but because religious life often lays upon us expectations that God never intends for us to meet. We soon discover that the expectations we think are from God are merely a human-made scaffolding that we think represents our identity and usefulness to the world.

When we rest, meditate, and seek God who loves us for who we are rather than for what we do, we feel useless and would rather be doing something else. That "something else" can become the high places God wants us to dismantle in the first place.

What does it take to move from "Woe is me?" to "Here I am, send me"? What does it take to dismantle the high places—the very scaffold of self-imposed expectations—in our life? It might not take such a vivid experience as Isaiah's vision of God in the throne room, but it does take the same kind of intimacy with God to find that your vocation was tailor-made just for you.

Too often, our distance from God makes God more like a dream than the Creator who is present with us every day. We experience God like a dream during our prayer time, but find that the dream fades away once we "re-enter" the world. The trick is to take God with us into the world well after we have left the prayer closets and sanctuaries of our lives; we take God with us when we utilize the gift and calling that God has upon our lives.

Ω

Shortly after Jesus' death and resurrection, during the time of the ancient Jewish holiday of Pentecost (Acts 2:1-21), Jesus sent the Holy Spirit to empower his disciples—men and women alike—to use their God-given gifts to build up God's people. The Bible explains that the Spirit came upon them like "tongues of fire." That fire, very much like the ember that touched Isaiah's lips, purified the disciples in order for the disciples to obey God's Word. God only had one expectation: be Good News in a world in which good news was hard to find, whether it meant giving to the poor or simply smiling at someone in the grocery line. No unrealistic expectations there!

Pentecost made all believers ministers, and like Isaiah we are called to live into our vocation of being caregiver and minister to those around us. We become prophets, pure and holy as the Lord is holy, not because of anything we accomplish, but because of God's grace upon our lives. God puts purpose to our steps, and sometimes it is only our unwillingness that keeps us from putting one foot in front of the other. Don't know where to start? More than likely, if you're a caregiver you've already started. Now it's a matter of letting God carry you the rest of the way and giving yourself permission to balance ministry to your loved ones with self-care.

Ω

In the early Christian church, monasteries became places in which men and women sought God in prayer, silence, work, and humility. It was in these hubs of the spirit in which people fashioned more contemporary ideas of vocation; that is, living a life devoted to God in ministry, compassion, and missions.

One important attribute that monasteries adopted is that of having a *rule of life*. It was St. Benedict who developed a rule for his monastic community and required certain regimens to be a part of his brothers' daily activities. To some, this kind of discipline can seem ritualistic at best and legalistic at worst. Yet, many monks and nuns throughout the centuries have found the Benedictine Rules empowering, spirit-filled, and liberating.

Rules help provide a framework and trellis for a spirit-filled life of discipline that brings order and normalcy to a hectic life. It is liberating because it relieves the guilt that often pervades questions surrounding vocation: Am I doing enough? Am I doing what God has asked? With a rule of life, both questions can be answered confidently and in the affirmative.

Rules of life have also been spiritually beneficial to a variety of communities. Martin Luther King, Jr., for instance, instituted a rule of life for the civil rights movement. In many ways, this non-violent ethic was the engine and catalyst that helped transform our very society. Other spiritual forefathers and foremothers of the faith, such as Dorothy Day and Gandhi, also had rules that structured their daily routine.

A rule of life is not an end but a means to an end. Rules help us focus on what is important in life, akin to the recommitment of vows that a married couple might make to one another. They also assist in varying the spiritual practices that a person includes in his or her spiritual diet. Most significantly, a rule of life brings together many spiritual disciplines that can help a believer be more Christ-like.

It is the loom that weaves a strong spiritual fabric that surrounds us, nurtures us, shapes and forms us, and inspires us. It helps us "draw near to God" as God draws near to us (James 4:8). Living a rule of life is worship to God and a basic structure for ordering our life around God's will and righteousness in our life.

The spiritual practice in this chapter does not emphasize Benedict's Rule or any specific rule for that matter; rather, the goal is to encourage you to develop a rule of life that works in your specific circumstances and brings balance to your vocation.

This is where readers synthesize, adopt, and adapt many, if not all, of the spiritual practices already discussed in this book. A tailor-made rule of life can bring joy and beneficial growth to anyone who aims to seek God in a daily, structured walk with the Spirit.

An example of a rule of life may include a certain time each day allotted for prayer, journaling, and scripture reading. It may also include weekly or monthly practices, such as fasting one day a week or month or abstaining from certain pleasures for a season, such as not watching television on certain week nights, and using that time for a spiritual practice. Also, keep in mind that rules may change and evolve over time as your journey unfolds with God.

Ω

Here is one such rule of life that incorporates many spiritual practices in this book:

I, [name], with the power and partnership of God's Holy Spirit, make a vow to:

- See my role as caregiver as a sacred vocation to which God has called me in this season of my life.

- Partner with my care receiver to ensure that all mutual respect and responsibility will be accomplished for God's glory.

- Be patient with myself and take time to care for myself.

- Replace guilt with prayer, fear with compassion, and anxiety with a sense of perspective.

- Nurture and practice spiritual disciplines that help me grow in my relationship with God, with my care receiver and with others.

- Take time to discern where God is working in my life, even when God seems distant.

As a result of this vow, I, [name], commit to:

- Praying for five minutes a day followed by two minutes of centering or silent prayer. (This time may expand as you become more comfortable with prayer and silence.)

- Journaling after supper three times a week and recording where I have experienced God in the past few days.

- Studying scripture for 15 minutes, twice a week.

- Practicing Sabbath rest for four hours on either a Saturday morning or Sunday afternoon, nap included.

- Exercising twice a week that incorporates "quiet time" [in other words, abstaining from music or electronic headsets] to allow for reflection, confession, expressions of gratitude, and meditation.

- Resting in silent meditation for 10 minutes a day.

Developing a rule of life does take some time and intentional forethought; but, ultimately, it is simple, smart, and savvy. Psalm 119 says, "Teach me, O Lord, the way of your statutes, and I will observe it to the end. Give me understanding, that I may keep your law and observe it with my whole heart" (vv. 33-34). Such rules can help us acknowledge our vocation and observe God's commands in a caregiver's daily life and unique journey.

Chapter Five Study Questions

1. Do you feel a call to be a caregiver?

2. Is that call empowering or overwhelming?

3. What keeps you from experiencing blessings in your role as caregiver?

4. In what ways do you experience God's leadership or guidance in your life?

Chapter 6: Grief Work with the Grieving God

Lazarus's Story

Jesus walked up the dirt path to Mary's and Martha's house. He felt the pang of hunger, the deep movement of exhaustion. The household was a solace, but it was a reminder that there was always more work to do.

Nothing reminded him more than Lazarus. Upon his arrival, Jesus looked deep into Lazarus's eyes, felt the sun-cracked skin of his handshake, felt the warm embrace of arms that took his cloak.

There was another time that Jesus saw Mary, Martha and Lazarus, but the situation was very different. That day was filled with grief and sorrow as Lazarus fell victim to a terminal illness.

Jesus travelled to Bethany to save his friend, but he arrived too late. And, rather than being greeted with the warm welcomes so familiar with Mary and Martha, he received tears and shouting: "Lord," Martha cried, "if you had been here, my brother would not have died" (John 11:21, 32).

Jesus replied out of habit with a word of hope, "I am the resurrection and the life." Even so, Jesus felt grief. He could not help but feel loss, for even if Lazarus rose from the dead, life would never be the same. It was only a foreshadowing of Jesus' own death. Jesus wept (John 11:35).

Jesus entered the home of this family and noticed how Lazarus had aged since that time. He felt the rush of sympathy for his friend, how that grief visited all of them at such an untimely hour. There was resurrection, but at a cost. The cost was the dark reminder that in Lazarus' death, Jesus saw his own fate. "Unless a grain of wheat falls to the earth and dies, it remains a single seed. But if it dies, it bears much fruit" (John 12:24).

Jesus smelled the bread, saw the table spread with food, heard Martha welcoming from the kitchen. A tear came to his eye yet again.

When Caregivers are Caregivers no More.

There are many resources that help caregivers cope with the stress of caregiving. Many relate to how to care for loved ones or how to make financial decisions; others help caregivers in the midst of hardship or pain. Few, however, address how to work and walk through the process of grief that comes when a caregiver loses a loved one.

Caregivers struggle with caring for loved ones, but what happens when a care receiver passes away? Like parents facing "empty nest syndrome" when a child moves out of the house, caregivers who lose loved ones must rediscover how to live into the grief, hardship, and eventual freedom that comes with moving beyond the caregiver role. Sometimes caregivers do not know who they *are* after the death of a loved one because their sense of identity, not to mention the role as caregiver, dies with their loved ones.

For other caregivers, this loss means being robbed of a life calling. Spouses who care for a loved one and then lose that loved one due to illness have a difficult time living life without having to care for their beloved around the clock. Other caregivers, such as adult children caring for parents, must discover the mixed grief of losing a parent and a person who may have consumed a great deal of time in any given day. Sure, the caregiver is no longer caregiving, but grief is a very real trouble for anyone who becomes that close to a loved one.

"Too many times we stand aside and let the waters slip away...dare to dance the tide" (Anonymous).

Losses, changes, transitions—good, bad, or indifferent—all bring about grieving. Some instances of loss, change, or transition affect our relationships because of death, illness, distance, work schedules, and even philosophies. Our relationships form the bases of our lives. We were created for community and when that community is disrupted, we grieve. With regard to the special relationship created between a caregiver and the person of whom they are taking care, this is especially true!

Grieving, despite its bad reputation, is a necessary part of growth and healing. Without the work of grieving, we tend to lose ourselves in the tangled emotional webs we weave. Grieving helps to gently untangle our needs, our fears, and our doubts from the truth of a change. Grieving helps us value and appreciate what went before and look forward to what is in store for us.

Ω

A few years ago, Daphne took a class on the Psalms at Columbia Theological Seminary. One of the assignments involved choosing a type of psalm (lament, happy, etc.) to write. The assignment elicited an inward groan from Daphne because she knew immediately what sort of psalm she needed to write: a lament. The idea of writing a lament was, on the surface, a simple one; yet underneath, an assignment that would pull from her difficult emotions surrounding her life and her relationship with God.

Yet, she wrote the psalm and it was indeed a lament. Now, one thing to know about laments: They are fluid. They move from anger and despair, through grace and mercy into joy. Daphne finds psalms of lament the most hopeful psalms. Her psalm dealt with the grief she experienced throughout her life, her ache for understanding the "why," and the ultimate mercy and solace found in God's presence throughout all of it.

In the stanzas of her psalm, Daphne compared grief to being on the beach and wondered if God was indeed the grief itself. *God is often said to be joy and love—why not grief?* If we began to experience our grief as yet one more way of being present with God, would the work be any easier? Would we be more in touch with the mercy and solace available to us through God's presence?

Late Catholic priest, Henri Nouwen, once noted that,

Jesus, the Blessed One, mourns. Jesus mourns when his friend Lazarus dies (see John 11:33-36); he mourns when he overlooks the city of Jerusalem, soon to be destroyed (see Luke 19:41-44). Jesus mourns over all losses and devastations that fill the human heart with pain. **He grieves with those who grieve and sheds tears with those who cry.**

The violence, greed, lust, and so many other evils that have distorted the face of the earth and its people causes [sic] the Beloved Son of God to mourn. **We too have to mourn if we hope to experience God's consolation.**[13] (Emphasis added.)

When Jesus goes to the Temple in Jerusalem and reads scripture, the scripture he reads is from Isaiah 61: 1-3:

The spirit of the Lord God is upon me,   because the Lord has anointed me; he has sent me to bring good news to the oppressed, **to bind up the brokenhearted***, to proclaim liberty to the captives, and release to the prisoners; to proclaim the year of the Lord's favor, and the day of vengeance of our God;* **to comfort all who mourn; to provide for those who mourn in Zion—to give them a garland instead of ashes, the oil of gladness instead of mourning, the mantle of praise instead of a**

---

[13] Henri J. M. Nouwen, *Bread for the Journey: A Daybook of Wisdom and Faith* (San Francisco: HarperOne, 1996): 153.

faint spirit. They will be called oaks of righteousness, the planting of the Lord, to display his glory. (Emphasis added.)

We hear Jesus tell the crowds gathered on the hillside that those who mourn will be comforted (Matt. 5:4).

We all live our lives in the presence of God. God is always present to the messiness of our lives.

Part of what we learn from studying Jesus' life is that Jesus experienced everything we experience. Jesus lived a human life, and he was very familiar with the losses and transitions through which we all live. The reason Jesus' life lessons are so important for us is that they create a sense of familiarity, of understanding, of acceptance — *of comfort.* There simply is nothing we can experience with which God has not become intimately acquainted. God comforts us with presence — just as we comfort those around us with our own presence in times of trouble, in times of grieving.

Ω

Grief is like a wave at the beach. Sometimes it roars in from way far out and knocks us down. Sometimes it sneaks in from just a little way out and pulls the sand from under our feet. Sometimes what looks like one of those waves that will surely knock us down actually dissipates before it ever reaches us.

If we look at each of these instances of grief and see God *as the grief*, how does that affect our experience of grief, of God?

Are there times in our journey through grief when we see God coming? Do we realize our feet are about to be knocked from under us? How about those times when we think we see God approaching only to feel a certain withdrawal, bringing a sort of disappointment with it. Through the varying depths and strengths of our experience of grief, God works with us in sorting out our issues, our questions, our needs, our desires. Coming to accept that God ensures we have what we need to do the work we need to do when we need to do it is possible. The role we have in this is openness and acceptance.

In looking back at Daphne's experience in the Psalms class and the practice of writing a lament, we find that the movement from lament through grace into joy was enlightening. By writing her own psalm, Daphne realized that she had lived through that movement time and again. In seeing it as such, the hope and comfort which kept her going was seen from a different perspective. God was seen as being an active participant and a companion on her journey. Indeed, God is the guiding presence in our lives which leads us through difficult periods and onto the high beach, safe from the rolling waves, to rest, to be comforted, to heal. We each have those high beaches in our lives. If God is present with us on those high beaches, then God is also present with us in the waves.

When considering God as actually being the waves of grief at that beach, perhaps we can experience a deeper sense of hope in the midst of our grieving. *When God is so deeply a part of the work we must do, then that work is good work, healing work, growth-inducing work.*

Chapter Six Study Questions

1. What grief are you living with in the midst of your caregiving?

2. How does your relationship with God speak to that grief and support you in your healing?

3. Scripture tells us that sorrow lasts for a night, but joy comes in the morning. What hints of joy has God put in your life?

Conclusion

Spiritual practices in the Christian life are as numerous as the qualities that make each caregiver unique. None of the practices will be for everyone, but surely many caregivers can discover a repertoire of daily spiritual exercises (even if only two or three) that helps draw them closer to Christ. These practices, when experienced over time with consistency and grace, form the loom that slowly draws all of life's threads into a beautiful tapestry of love.

Caregivers often feel alone in this process, but they are not. As they weave their tapestry of love on a spirit-inspired loom, they join a Restless Weaver that supports them in their work and rest. A hymn penned by O. I. Cricket Harrison, entitled *Restless Weaver*, expresses God's participation in this journey. The fourth stanza is an appropriate one for us who care for loved ones:

Restless Weaver, still conceiving new life – now and yet to be – binding all your vast creation in one living tapestry:

You have called us to be weavers. Let your love guide all we do. With your Reign of Peace our pattern, we will weave your world anew.[14]

---

[14] Daniel Merrick and David Polk, eds. *Chalice Hymnal* (St. Luis: Chalice Press, 1995), p. 658.

Over the past six chapters, we have been discussing only a handful of the most popular of practices that can form a sufficient and rich tapestry. Some are easier to employ than others, but none of them should produce guilt if they are neither accomplished nor mastered.

The goal is not to set up another set of demands, another to-do list. The loom, no matter how it looks, intends to set each caregiver's heart in a direction that takes him or her to God and to do so with a resource that provides a larger vision for the caregiver role.

Let us not forget that loss and grief will always be a part of the journey as well. We humans are a fragile species, and we confront the sting of death all too often. It is, after all, the last and greatest enemy God has yet to defeat. With a tapestry of love in place, however, even our thickest darkness and deepest despair can be managed easily in a web of care and divine providence. That tapestry has the potential to be a strong one. It has the potential to be a vibrant, life-giving one. It has the potential to enrapture our lives with renewed hope, a sense of vision, a purpose for the day, and strength for the road ahead.

So, with that, we leave you with a prayer of encouragement and support, a prayer that we hope will provide much-needed strength for your journey ahead:

Restless Weaver, who weaves a tapestry of love that envelops us all:

Bring the Spirit of life and light to our table, enlightening all our journeys, and let your Bread of Life fill us with nourishment, quench our spiritual thirst, and fill our cups with courage and insight.

Bless us with the audacity of Martha and empower us to make a sacred space for You.

Bless us with the patience of Mary, remembering that it is appropriate to stop, listen, wait, learn and reflect when You ask us to do so.

Bless us with the mind of Christ, which brings peace and clarity from the perspective of the baptized, resurrected, and renewed life.

For it is in His Name we pray. Amen.

Appendix A:

Historic Spiritual Practices for a life well-lived.

There are a variety of spiritual practices and disciplines that help Christians grow in their relationship with Christ; however, we encourage Christians who engage in spiritual practices to keep in mind several rules of thumb.

We encourage you to approach the content of this book differently than you would any other. Many readers read non-fiction to glean information. This book, however, encourages *formational* reading, which is a spiritual practice in and of itself. Formational reading requires that we begin in a spirit of humility and openness. We pray for God's voice to speak through the words of the text and excavate that which God desires to share in the reading of the text. Reading *formationally* is not a "quick study" approach. Time needs to be set aside; a quiet place found. Those who come to the text are encouraged to read slowly and listen for words that resonate with the heart or spirit. As that occurs, having a journal or a pad of paper nearby becomes important. You may choose to write in the margins, taking notes on how the text moved, touched, or spoke to you. This is essential to the *formative* nature of reading a text.

Sometimes, whatever has made itself known through the text is enough to stop us for the time being. When that happens, we encourage you to see it as a sign of God's love and attention. Responding to what God has shared, as well as how strongly it is felt, is part of the process. As unbelievable as it sounds, when we are prepared to receive a word, even twenty minutes of reading will be inspiring and formative.

A word about journaling: When we approach the discipline of journaling with a prayerfully open heart, deep spiritual work can take place. As the first thought makes its way onto the page, a breath is taken, and another thought follows. Journaling is habit-forming! How you choose to journal depends on your preferred writing style. Your journal can be in a pretty, bound book; it can consist simply of a spiral bound notebook, a legal pad, online blog, or word processor.

The most important aspect in journaling is to have firm boundaries about the access other people have to it. *Be sure to have others leave it alone.* This ensures that you can write honestly and know that no one else will read it. Another aspect is to write regularly. Many folks write in a stream-of-consciousness manner, while others write in letter or narrative form. Some simply jot down words or phrases; others draw or sketch their thoughts instead. However you decide to express yourself and record thoughts, *the prayerful regularity of journaling is what makes the process a spiritual discipline.*

As a companion to prayer, journaling can be a way of recording the names of others for whom we pray, the issues we are addressing in prayer either for ourselves or others, and the blessings we find in the answers to those prayers we offer up as they are revealed to us. There is more information on effective journaling in the first chapter.

Prayer, as its own spiritual practice, is the one that embraces all the others. Little to no prayer might impede an open heart and mind. When preparatory prayer is not present, the work of the loom, the strengthening structure for our spiritual journey, is faulty and weak. Therefore, pray! Pray without ceasing, and especially before engaging in any spiritual discipline.

Silence and *solitude* can aid us in our prayer life. *Solitude* is the discipline of spending time without any others or any distractions. Silence, a frequent companion to solitude, is simply the discipline of having no external noise or conversation. Silence and solitude are good precursors for prayer.

Another spiritual discipline is that of *fasting*. When we think of fasting, we usually think of abstaining from food or drink for a certain period of time. The Israelites, as well as the early church, observed fasting as a private discipline. Within the Sermon on the Mount, Jesus says,

> *And whenever you fast, do not look dismal, like the hypocrites, for they disfigure their faces so as to show others that they are fasting. Truly I tell you, they have received their reward. But when you fast, put oil on your head and wash your face, so that your fasting may be seen not by others but by your Father who is in secret; and your Father who sees in secret will reward you (Matthew 6:16-18).*

Also, *fasting* meant eating and drinking *enough.* Being very mindful of what is set before us to eat and eating only that amount which satisfies us provides us with the nourishment needed to do the work we are called to do. However, in the spirit of hospitality, if one is entertaining a traveler, then it is customary to eat with the stranger so that the stranger feels comfortable and welcome. When a feast day or other community celebration is held, another aspect of the fasting custom is to participate by eating enough so that *attention is* not *drawn* to one's fasting.

Fasting is a discipline in which mindfulness of what we eat is present as well as an awareness of when and why we eat. The discipline of fasting from those things and activities which consume us is becoming more popular and can be a productive way of looking more carefully at our lives.

Frugality, as another spiritual discipline, is a way of using resources for purposes outside our own needs for a time. Some look upon frugality with suspicion when it is suggested by a church. That said, we must ask how often we seriously consider doing without a dinner out so another family might simply have dinner. How often do we stop and think about ways of saving money? Yet, *why* are we saving that money? What is it that we are going to spend it on?

Sacrifice is a discipline complementary to frugality and is one which allows you to stretch your sense of what you can do without for the sake of those who have less. Most of the time, we begin with developing a sense of sacrifice and end up living a more frugal life, which is an example of the growth the discipline of living spiritual practices can achieve.

Secrecy or *confidentiality* is simply the discipline of doing good deeds or making offerings without allowing anyone to know about the deeds you do or the money you give. This keeps us from giving for the wrong reasons. Only God needs to know. Most caregivers are actually experts at this spiritual discipline because of the work being done day in and day out for their care receivers. So, consider looking at a typical day in your household, and be aware of the good deeds and offerings you are doing without any fanfare. Reviewing our lives in this manner is an excellent way of looking at where we are in our spiritual growth.

Study is a discipline in which you may memorize Scripture and expand your universe of biblical study helps. Reading for spiritual formation, to which we referred earlier, is what study is all about. Study is not about reading like we once did in school; rather, it's about letting God's word take root deep within our hearts and produce a bountiful, life-giving harvest of knowledge and wisdom.

Worship is a spiritual discipline which happens when we express our faith by offering praise and thanksgiving to god, by asking for god's blessings and grace, and by responding to god in compassion and holiness. During worship recently, when Daphne's daughter was having difficulty settling down, she offered the belief that God is with us all the time, every day. One day a week, we gather with others to be with God as a community. We pray together, sing together, and hear scripture read and interpreted together. Daphne explained that a community of faith is the embodiment of Christ in the world today and that we derive strength from this time together so that on all the other days, we can hear and see God and do what God wants of us.

Nor does community have to occur within the confines of a church building. Community may be found in the living room, in the activities room in the apartment building, or in the gathering spaces of our lives. Worship happens when we gather with others to hear and reflect on God's Word. Where can that happen in your life if getting to church on Sunday morning is not possible? How can worship take place with your care receiver?

Celebration is the discipline of being grateful both in your own relationship with Christ and with other believers. Celebration is the expression of encouragement to and gratitude for others. Many people begin their journey by keeping a gratitude journal. Such a spiritual practice is a wonderful way of staying aware of God's generous actions in our lives.

Service is the discipline of giving your time to a community and/or to others. Ponder tithing your time. Giving your time to someone else might seem a little overwhelming; however, opening our hearts to those outside of our normal activities opens our lives to even more of God's grace! Service can be enriching to the spiritual journey because as a discipline, it takes us out of ourselves. When we are open to God's grace and are focused outward, amazing things happen to our hearts, minds, and relationships.

Fellowship is a discipline in which we gather for reasons other than worship. Hebrews 10:24-25 states, "And let us consider how to provoke one another to love and good deeds, not neglecting to meet together, as is the habit of some, but encouraging one another, and all the more as you see the Day approaching." Christians are called to be a community. When we live in a community, we are active with the other members of that community. Gathering for coffee or a meal, for a walk and a talk, even for a movie with those with whom we share worship, deepens our experience of Christ.

Confession is the discipline of confessing sins to trusted people who are spiritual allies that provide prayerful support. James 5:16 reminds us to, "Confess your sins to one another and pray for one another, that you may be healed." The walking and talking of fellowship can sometimes invite a spiritual closeness which would open the door for confession. Always consider feelings of desired confidentiality when either listening to or giving a confession. Most of the time, however, we look to our pastors, deacons, and even chaplains for this type of time and attention.

Submission is the discipline of giving up our desires for those of God. Submission is also about giving up what we desire or something we think we should do in favor of what someone else desires or thinks should be done. Although submission may be misused and abused by churches, care receivers, abusive spouses, and by those in power (especially to condone violence against women and minorities), true biblical submission is a liberating discipline. In fact, submitting to the proper people in appropriate ways is a good way to fight against sin and pride.

The discipline of submission is perhaps one of the most difficult to truly practice. Caregiving, however, is a perfect field for the discipline of a healthy type of submission to emerge: Within the caregiving situation, to whom should we be willing to submit? Think of how hard it is for some of us to allow others to help and all the reasons we tend to offer for that refusal—could those be avenues of submission for us as caregivers? Think of how often we argue with the ones for whom we care, arguments over issues that are not crucial to the person's safety or our own. Is it possible to allow the other person to be right some times?

A lot of times, in our struggles to maintain control of a situation that appears to be out of control, we lose sight of compassion; we allow our view to become the one that is always the most correct, efficacious, or even fun. By participating in the discipline of submission, a lightness of *being* may enter into our souls because of the lifting of the heavy shroud of responsibility that comes with always being right, always being the one to make the decisions—all those attitudes that add to caregiving burdens!

Appendix B:
Works Cited and Suggested Reading

Arnold, Johann Christoph. *Why Forgive?* Maryknoll: Orbis Books, 2009.

Badcock, Gary. *The Way of Life: A Theology of Christian Vocation.* Grand Rapids: Wm. B. Eerdmans, 1998.

Chittister, Joan. *The Rule of Benedict: Insights for the Ages.* New York: Crossroads, 1992.

Collins, Pat. *Prayer in Practice: A Biblical Approach.* Maryknoll: Orbis Books, 2001.

Dahill, Lisa. *Truly Present: Practicing Prayer in the Liturgy.* Minneapolis: Augsburg Fortress Press, 2005.

de Waal, Esther. *Seeking God: The Way of St. Benedict.* Collegeville (MN): The Liturgical Press, 2001.

Fischer, Kathleen. *Forgiving Your Family: A Journey to Healing.* Nashville: Upper Room Books, 2005.

Funk, Mary Margaret. *Humility Matters for Practicing the Spiritual Life.* New York: Continuum, 2010.

_____. *Thoughts Matter: The Practice of the Spiritual Life.* New York: Continuum, 1998.

_____. *Tools Matter for Practicing the Spiritual Life.* New York: Continuum, 2004.

Gill-Austern, Brita. "Love Understood as Self-Sacrifice and Self-Denial: What Does It Do to Women? In *Through the Eyes of Women: Insights for Pastoral Care,* ed. Jeanne Stevenson Moessner. Minneapolis: Fortress Press, 1996: 304-321.

Guberman, Nancy, Pierre Maheu and Chantal Maille. "Women as Family Caregivers: Why Do They Care?" *The Gerontologist* 32:5 (October 1992): 607-617.

Guthrie, Suzanne. *Grace's Window: Entering the Season of Prayer*. New York: Morehouse Publishing, 2008.

Hamma, Robert M. *Prayers of Renewal and Restoration in Times of Caregiving*. Notre Dame: Ave Marie Press, 2004.

Keating, Thomas. *Invitation to Love: The Way of Christian Contemplation*. New York: Continuum, 1994.

May, Melanie. "One Woman's Wrestling with Vocation." *Brethren Life and Thought* 46 (March 2004): 231-236.

McLeod, Beth. *Caregiving: The Spiritual Journey of Love, Loss and Renewal*. New York: John Wiley and Sons, Inc., 1999.

Merrick, Daniel, and David Polk, eds. *Chalice Hymnal*. St. Luis: Chalice Press, 1995.

Mulholland, M. Robert. *Invitation to a Journey: A Road Map for Spiritual Formation*. Downers Grove: InterVarsity Press, 1993.

Muller, Wayne. *Sabbath: Finding Rest, Renewal, and Delight in Our Busy Lives*. New York: Bantam, 1999.

Nouwen, Henri J. M. *Bread for the Journey: A Daybook of Wisdom and Faith*. San Francisco: HarperOne, 1996.

Saliers, Don. *Worship and Spirituality*. Maryville (TN): OSL Publications, 1996.

Shelly, Judith Allen. *Spiritual Care: A Guide for Caregivers*. Downers Grove: InterVarsity Press, 2000.

Thompson, Marjorie J. *Soul Feast*. Louisville: Westminster John Knox Press, 1995.

_____. *The Way of Forgiveness*. Nashville: Upper Room Books, 2002.

Tutu, Desmond. *No Future Without Forgiveness.* New York: Image Book/Doubleday, 2000.

Wingren, Gustaf. *Luther on Vocation.* Trans. by Carl C. Rasmussen. Philadelphia: Muhlenberg Press, 1957.

Wuellner, Flora Slosson. *Forgiveness: The Passionate Journey.* Nashville: Upper Room Books, 2001.

Made in the USA
Lexington, KY
24 November 2014